Federalist Thinking

Lucio Levi

UNIVERSITY PRESS OF AMERICA,® INC.
Lanham • Boulder • New York • Toronto • Plymouth, UK

Copyright © 2008 by
University Press of America,® Inc.
4501 Forbes Boulevard
Suite 200
Lanham, Maryland 20706
UPA Acquisitions Department (301) 459-3366

Estover Road
Plymouth PL6 7PY
United Kingdom

Library of Congress Control Number: 2007936544
ISBN-13: 978-0-7618-3922-4 (paperback : alk. paper)
ISBN-10: 0-7618-3922-4 (paperback : alk. paper)

Originally published as:
Il pensiero federalista

In series:
Biblioteca Essenziale Laterza, 47
Gius. Laterza & Figli Spa
Roma-Bari
© 2002

English version edited by Lionello Casalegno and Lucio Levi

U.S. reference
Joseph Preston Baratta

Table of Contents

Introduction

The first significant appearance of federalism in history dates back to the Philadelphia Convention, which in 1787 drafted the Constitution of the United States of America. When it first appeared, federalism was the theory of a new form of government, devised to solve the problems of an isolated case, the setting up of the United States. For a long time it remained a marginal political model, if one considers that until World War Two only three other states had adopted a federal Constitution: Switzerland (1848), Canada (1867) and Australia (1901). It is to be noted that these federations were established in peripheric regions of the world, far from the propelling centres of world politics. The prevailing form of political organization at the time was the unitary state, based on the national ideology. Its structure was quite suitable for ensuring a strong internal cohesion between classes and regions, essential for assuring the state survival in a world of sovereign nations in permanent conflict among them. That international political climate, full of tensions, could not remain without consequences on the federal institutions. They too underwent a centralist degeneration, mostly in the time of the world wars.

Only after the end of World War Two did federalism progressively expand its coverage, up to assuming the character of a movement of world dimensions. It will suffice to mention that two multinational states of very large dimensions—India, after having achieved its political independence, and Russia, after the fall of the Soviet regime—have adopted constitutions that come close to the federal model. In Europe, the continent which has exported to the rest of the world the political formula of the national state, a process of supranational unification is under way, which has already led to the formation of pre-federal institutions like the European Parliament or the European Central Bank.

The process is accompanied by the tendency to institute regional and local self-governments, which has grown in an uneven fashion: in some states it went as far as forming federal (Germany and Belgium) or quasi-federal (Austria) institutions, in others it has taken the form of regional autonomies (Italy and Spain), but it is active in France also, where the opposition to such a reorganization of institutions is stronger, due to its centralist tradition.

These processes represent an answer to the agony of the national state and are the expression of the tendency to create new forms of statehood with a federative character, which overcome the national state model from above and from below, and create new levels of government above nations and inside them.

Finally, the globalization process is eroding the sovereignty of every state, even the most powerful, and poses the problem of enlarging the state's orbit in order to make it adequate to cope with the global dimensions taken by the main problems in economy, environment, security, social justice and human-rights protection. The trend is, in other words, to progressively overcome the division of humanity in sovereign states and to transform the UN into a system of federal world government.

The new character assumed by federalism after World War Two appears most clearly in the European unification process. It has to be noted, first of all, that the promoters of federal processes in the past were sharing with the supporters of national unifications the objective to create new sovereign states, and were willing to accept the division of the world in sovereign states as an inevitable fact. They could not avoid in any way the political and military pressure that the other states were exerting on the federation's borders, hence they were driven to strengthen their central government with mighty bureaucratic and military apparatuses, put to the service of their security and power needs. Instead, the European unification places itself in a new chapter of history, that of a growing interdependence between peoples and states, which has recently reached its peak in the globalization process, at the conclusion of which the overcoming of the division of humankind in sovereign states is foreshadowed. In such a perspective the European federation appears to be the first stage of a federative process bound to culminate in the federal unification of the world.

Despite its amazing success and diffusion, that was coincidental with the rooting of influential federalist movements in Europe and in the world, the place that federalism occupies in the history of political thought is not clearly defined. On the one hand, there is a clear, but reductive, definition, namely that federalism would be the theory of a particular type of state: the federal state or a federation of states. It is a theory of a constitutional character, according to which the specific aspect of federalism would be the division of power in two government levels (the central power and the federated communities' power), and starting from this datum builds the theory of federal institutions.

On the other hand, there is the tendency to conceive federalism as a broader theory, of which the institutional dimension represents only one aspect, and which intends to give its own answer to the problems of society, economy and history. According to such a viewpoint, federalism would then be an ideology, i.e. a comprehensive conception of political life, like liberalism or socialism. However, if one considers the best-known attempt to look at federalism in such a perspective, that by Proudhon, one has to acknowledge that his is an unsatisfactory definition, because it is not founded on a scientific approach to the analysis of the social structure and it has an historically undefined character. Only recently efforts have been made to give a definition of federalism in more theoretically-rigorous terms.

The need to proceed in the exposition of the history of federal thinking on the solid ground of data that lend themselves to be seen and described in clear conceptual terms, suggests that we start from that dialectical set of theories and political actions which led to the birth of the United States of America, the first example in history of a federal pact among sovereign states and at the same time the most important, although only partially developed, constitutional experience in the history of federal institutions. The federal government has been the subject of many analyses—the first and most famous of which is, as we will see, *The Federalist*—, that have thoroughly illustrated its structure and functions. Therefore, it does not constitute an argument liable to produce deeply diverging interpretations. The analysis of its constitutional model allows us to come to a first description of federalist theory, and we will then proceed from what is clear and non-controversial to what is less clear and still problematic.

Typesetting has been paid for by the Department of Political Studies of the University of Torino.

Chapter One

The Federalist and the Constitution of the United States of America

1.1 THE PHILADELPHIA CONVENTION AND THE INVENTION OF FEDERAL INSTITUTIONS

The British colonies of North America, which after the Revolution became thirteen independent republics, joined in an association with a bond of a confederal type. The Philadelphia Convention, setting the first example in history of a federal pact among sovereign states, gave birth to a new kind of state, whose functioning mechanism was described in the essays of *The Federalist*, drafted by Alexander Hamilton (1755–1804), John Jay (1745–1829) and James Madison (1751–1836) in 1787–88 with the aim of showing the superiority of the federal system over the confederal.

In what sense the birth of the United States represents a political novelty? It is so in at least two aspects. First of all, it is the establishment of a new state, formed, unlike what had always happened before, through a democratic procedure and not by act of force. Second, with the new state a new form of power organization was created, never experimented before, the first Federation in history.

The political unification of a group of states, although a relatively not very frequent event in the course of history, certainly was not a new fact. What is new, or rather "prodigious", to use Hamilton's expression, is the unification of a group of republican states accomplished not by war, but by a democratic procedure. The Constitution, in fact, was submitted for ratification to assemblies expressly elected in the States, applying the revolutionary principle written down in the Declaration of Independence, according to which "it is the right of the People [. . .] to institute new Government."

Let us read what Hamilton wrote: "The establishment of a Constitution, in time of profound peace, by the voluntary consent of a whole people, is

1

a PRODIGY, to the completion of which I look forward with trembling anxiety" (*The Federalist No. 85*). Tocqueville did grasp very clearly this novelty of the formation of the United States. He argued that all ages have furnished the spectacle of a people struggling with energy to win its independence.

> But what is new in the history of societies is to see a great people turn a calm and scrutinizing eye upon itself when apprised by the legislature that the wheels of its government are stopped, to see it carefully examine the extent of the evil, and patiently wait two whole years until a remedy is discovered, to which voluntarily submitted, without its costing a tear or a drop of blood from mankind (Tocqueville A., 117–18).

Hamilton, in the first page of *The Federalist,* says more. He thus defines the meaning of the constitutional choice facing the peoples of the East Coast of North America:

> It has been frequently remarked that it seems to have been reserved to the people of this country, by their conduct and example, to decide the important question whether societies of men are really capable or not of establishing good government from reflection and choice, or whether they are forever destined to depend for their political constitutions on accident and force" (*The Federalist No. 1*).

Until then, the foundation of States had been the result of "accident" and "force." But in America, at the dawn of the democratic era, the possibility had arisen for the first time to found a State basing this event on "reflection" and free "choice."

In the Founding Fathers there is the pride of having been able not only to innovate the organizational forms of political societies for the good of Americans, but also to create a political model that the rest of humanity could benefit from. "But why is the experiment of an extended republic to be rejected, merely because it may comprise what is new?", Madison asks himself, and replies: "To this manly spirit, posterity will be indebted for the possession, and the world for the example, of the numerous innovations displayed on the American theatre, in favor of private rights and public happiness." Madison proudly claims the Founding Fathers' right to innovate.

> Happily for America, happily, we trust, for the whole human race, they pursued a new and more noble course. They accomplished a revolution which has no parallel in the annals of human society. They reared the fabrics of governments which have no model on the face of the globe (*The Federalist No. 14*).

In these two sentences of the two major authors of the *Federalist Papers* we can feel the excitement of the Founding Fathers of the United States before the invention of federalism. They reveal the effort these men are doing in defining the nature of that exceptional political change of which they are at the same time spectators and actors.

Unlike the biggest States in the world (Russia, China, India), which are the heirs of big empires, the United States has shown that federal institutions allow for vast territories to be unified through the democratic method. The US Constitution represented a break in the expansionist and imperialist tradition that had always been governing the formation of new States.

The Federalist is an exemplary text of the new democratic era, which has brought with it a profound change in the way political action is conceived of. On the one hand, democracy requires that the plans of politicians be submitted to the screening of public opinion, whose judgment is the necessary, although not sufficient, guarantee that political decisions correspond to people's interests. The confrontation between politicians and public opinion is based on a rational dialogue between equals seeking truth and the common good. After peoples stormed the stage of politics, history has attained such a level of maturity that political action is no longer by necessity unaware of its consequences. It tends to become a process subject to human planning. On the other hand, the great political events that determine the course of history, like the establishment of new States, are no longer the works of "cosmic-historical" individuals, as Hegel would say (Moses, Theseus, Cyrus), but tend to become collective undertakings. In fact, in America, for the first time in history, the people was summoned to determine, and confirm with their vote, a great collective choice—the Constitution—which was to regulate the form of their political living-together for many generations.

Hamilton quotes on this subject a telling reflection by Hume, guide and master of the authors of *The Federalist*:

> "To balance a large state or society [says he], whether monarchical or republican, on general laws, is a work of so great difficulty, that no human genius, however comprehensive, is able, by the mere dint of reason and reflection, to effect it. The judgments of many must unite in the work; EXPERIENCE must guide their labor; TIME must bring it to perfection, and the FEELING of inconveniences must correct the mistakes which they inevitably fall into in their first trials and experiments" (*The Federalist No. 85*).

The Philadelphia Convention represented the attempt to create new political institutions, or rather a new State, based on free, rational choice. The delegates to the Convention were men with a very-high-level political culture. As the French economic-affairs-attaché Hector St. John de Crèvecoeur wrote, "the Convention was composed of the continent's most enlightened men" (Warren C., 370). And Jefferson defined the Convention nothing less than "an assembly of semi-gods" (Cappon L.J. ed., 196, vol. 1).

However, the Constitution it drafted does not correspond to a previously-conceived political design. This confirms that the decisions that steered the direction of that historic process were the result of the clashing of different and diverging wills. The Constitution was the result of a set of compromises between the political breaking off from the Empire and the continuity with the British juridical tradition; between federal sovereignty and States sovereignty; between big and small States; between proportional representation of the people and equal representation of the States; between federalists, who were supporting institutional reform as a means for defeating anarchy and re-pelling the interference of European powers, and anti-federalists, who were afraid that a federal government would threaten the liberties acquired with the revolution; between the economy of the North, composed of independent farmers, and of the South, based on plantations and slave labor; between the North's manufacturing vocation and protectionist policy and the Southern States' agricultural, plantations-based economy, relying on exports and free trade with Britain.

The agreement on the new form of government came from a compromise between two political currents. The first wanted a unitary State which had to get rid of the sovereignty of the thirteen States, the second wanted a better-ment of the Confederation with no limitations to the sovereignty of the thir-teen States. But nobody had envisaged a plan for a Federation. Until then, the model of the unitary State was the only paradigm in existence that allowed people to understand and control political life.

At first, also the authors of *The Federalist* belonged in the unitary current. Hamilton had worked out a project which drew inspiration from the British Constitution. Also the supporters of the Confederation were still attached to the unitary-State model and started from the idea that one shall not (and could not) limit the States' sovereignty.

Only in one sense is it possible to say that the unitary current prevailed over the particularist: it succeeded in imposing the creation of one State compris-ing the thirteen States of North America. But the form of that State differed from the original project of the supporters of political unification. The State's federal form was the result of the influence exerted on the course of events by the anti-federalists, who got the point of maintaining the independence of the States.

Hence, it is possible to say that federalism was not a doctrine pre-existing the Constitution. Before the Constitution there was neither federalism nor federalists, but at the most ideas forerunning federalism. "Commentators of the Constitution who have read the *Federalist*, instead of reading the debates held before it", Carl Warren wrote, "have ascribed to the Founding Fathers the invention of a sublime concept called 'Federalism' [. . .] Federalism, as the doctrine is generally known, was an improvisation, which was later promoted to political doctrine" (Warren C., 804).

It is not an exaggeration to speak of improvisation, because the new often comes to life all of a sudden under the thrust of circumstances that men cannot master. The Constitution's form, albeit it was partly the result of rational discussions, did indeed partly have an accidental character.

The theory of the federal State and the federalist doctrine were born after the Philadelphia Convention, as a reflection about the new institutions that nobody wanted or anticipated. To ideology, and in particular to the federalist ideology, the same comment can be applied that Hegel addresses to philosophy.

> Philosophy, as the thought of the world, does not appear until reality has completed its formative process, and made itself ready. History thus corroborates the teaching of the conception that only in the maturity of reality does the ideal appear as counterpart to the real, apprehends the real world in its substance, and shapes it into an intellectual kingdom. It appears for the first time after some time, when reality has accomplished its formation process [. . .] The ideal appears in front of reality in the maturity of reality (Hegel G.W.F., 2001, 20).

And Marx, with a similar formula, but in a philosophical perspective that pretends to have the key for changing the world, rather than limiting itself to interpreting it, wrote that

> "Mankind inevitably sets itself only such tasks as it is able to solve, since closer examination will always show that the problem itself arises only when the material conditions for its solution are already present or at least in the course of formation." (Marx K., *A Contribution to the Critique of Political Economy. Preface*, 265).

It is an abstract way of conceiving history the one according to which the solution precedes the problem. History always poses new problems, and solutions push their way along a path that is not laid out in advance, but penetrates in unexplored regions. If it is true that awareness is a product of history, or, in other terms, it is a reflection on the problems posed by history, it is also true that history, being innovation, is a product of awareness.

Federal institutions are an American invention. Like any constitutional model which was useful in solving important problems of political life, they have had a big influence in the world and have been widely imitated. The

Federalist is the expression of one of those privileged moments when the spark flashes of a new awareness of the historic significance of an institutional innovation: the invention of a very powerful instrument of government which humanity can use for controlling the historical process.

It was not the Founding Fathers who coined the word defining the new form of government. It was not, as we have seen, the result of a preconceived plan, but of the compromise between political groups who wanted something different from the Constitution. Thus, after the Constitution had come into force, the necessity to give the language a univocal meaning imposed the custom to denote the new State by the name Federation. From then on it was possible to realize that the Constitution had given birth to a State whose novelty was that it had not eliminated the member-States' independence. In fact, the Federation, according to Hamilton's definition, is "an association of two or more states into one state" (*The Federalist No. 9*). This State-form took the name of Federation thanks also to the influence exerted by *The Federalist*, which was the first commentary to the Constitution, while the custom to indicate by the name of Confederation the old organizational form, namely the permanent league among the States, consolidated.

1.2 THE THEORY OF FEDERAL INSTITUTIONS

The Federalist is not only the first commentary to the Constitution of the United States, written when it had not yet entered into force. It contains also the first formulation of the theory of the federal State. For sure it is not a systematic exposition. In any case, that could not be possible, given that the authors of *The Federalist* had in front of them a draft of the Constitution of which they were warmly supporting the approval. It was not even sure (hence the "trembling anxiety" expressed by Hamilton in the last article of *The Federalist*) that the Constitution would receive the people's consent and, in case it did, whether the Federation would stand the test of time. They did not have that ample panorama that allows us today to make comparative analyses, and gives us the empirical material necessary for working out a theory of the federal institutions.

On the other hand, the aim the authors of *The Federalist* had was first of all to disprove the objections of the anti-federalists and persuade the readers to support the Constitution. Many questions escaped their consideration, whose relevance has been highlighted by the historical experience of federal institutions, not only in the United States; first of all the question of the legitimacy of secession, which is not dealt with in *The Federalist*. As everybody knows, only after the Secession War will the Supreme Court decree, with its ruling in the *Texas versus White* case of 1868, that the Constitution does not contemplate the right of secession among the States' rights.

At this point we have the elements that allow us to define the essential features of federal institutions. When Hamilton dealt with this difficult problem, mostly in the 9th and 15th chapters of *The Federalist Papers*, he underlined two aspects of the problem. Firstly, as we have seen above, he defined the Federation as "an association of two or more states into one state." In this way, he identified the novelty of federal institutions in their attributing a state-like character to both the Union and member states. The two orders of power must therefore be considered equal and independent each in its own sphere.

Secondly, he underlined the fact that with the Constitution the government of the Union had acquired a direct power over the citizens. Whereas what is peculiar to the Confederation is "the principle of LEGISLATION for STATES or GOVERNMENTS" (*The Federalist No. 15*), a Federation permits to "extend the authority of the Union to the persons of the citizens" (*The Federalist No. 15*). And this is a power that the Federation shares with the states, because they too continue to directly exert their power towards individuals. The Federation's intricate nature consists in the fact, then, that it is a political community composed at the same time of states and individuals.

Certainly, the acquisition by the federal government of a direct power over the citizens and, vice-versa, the direct participation of the citizens in the election of the federal authorities were the most important changes that marked the formation of the Federation. However, that feature of the federal institutions still does not let us appreciate the difference between a Federation and a unitary state with regional autonomies. Indeed, also the regions of a decentralized unitary state have a direct power over individuals. However, the relation that is established in a Federation between federal government and federated states is not of a hierarchical nature, but is a division of powers "between co-ordinate and independent authorities." This is the peculiar aspect of federal institutions, as Albert V. Dicey defined it in its *Introduction to the Study of the Law of the Constitution* (151).

The new constitutional principle on which the federal state is based is the division of power in two institutional levels: that of the federal government and that of the federated states. And even Hamilton, who had initially sided in favor of a strong unitary government, accepted the federal Constitution and supported it without any reservation in the ratifying Convention of the state of New York, because he understood that the powers granted to the federal government were sufficient to eliminate the cause of political and economic disorder in the North American continent and to assure to Americans a destiny of peace, democracy and prosperity for many generations to come.

In the time of the American Revolution there was an idea that had a universal following: that in every state, power must be concentrated in one centre. This viewpoint was common to both those intending to retain the Constitution, and those intending to amend it. That opinion lived on even after the entry into force of the Constitution.

For instance, John C. Calhoun (1782–1850), the constitutionalist who provided the theoretical basis for the secessionist initiative of the Southern states, took into examination the US government structure, and, moving from the postulate of sovereignty's indivisibility, came to the conclusion that sovereignty belongs to the States, because they have never surrendered it. Hence the Union's government was subordinate to the states and they were entitled to the right of secession, the right to unilaterally annul federal laws and the right to paralyse the coercive action of the federal government. This means, according to Calhoun, that the federal pact is no different from any international treaty.

Should the essential features of the Constitution really be those illustrated by this theory, the conclusion to draw would be that the Philadelphia Constitution did not produce any significant institutional innovation. Actually, the difficulty to rigorously define the institutional innovation contained in the federal Constitution still remains to this day, mostly on the question whether sovereignty in a Federation is divisible or not. Federal Constitutions define the distribution of power between the federal government and the federated states so that these maintain some pristine prerogatives, in particular an independent power in a limited, but well-defined number of sectors. Similarly, the federal government has limited, but real powers in other sectors.

In the ratification assembly of the state of New York, Hamilton addressed with great clarity this problem.

> That two supreme powers cannot act together, is false. They are inconsistent only when they are aimed at each other, or at one indivisible object. The laws of the United States are supreme, as to all their proper, constitutional objects; the laws of the states are supreme in the same way. These supreme laws may act on different objects without clashing, or they may operate on different parts of the same object, with perfect harmony" (Hamilton A., 103, vol. 5).

Hence, every point of the territory and every individual belong at the same time to two states (the member state and the federal state) which are coordinated with each other so that a unitary decision on every problem can always be reached.

The novelty of federal institutions lies in the fact that power distribution is organized in such a way that some power centres have the last word in some matters, others in others, without establishing hierarchical relationships between different powers. This does not mean that in a Federation sovereignty is divided, as the authors of *The Federalist* argue. The aforementioned difficulty arises from the fact that in analysing federal institutions only two elements are usually considered: the federal government and the states governments. Actually, as Hans Kelsen suggests, the Federation is composed of three elements: the federal government, the state governments and the two of them as a whole, that is to say the Federation (Kelsen H., 1999, 316–19). Then it becomes clear that the title to sovereignty must be ascribed to the Federation.

One comes to the same conclusion starting from the postulate of popular sovereignty and considering that in a Federation the people has a plural character, expressing itself in a double citizenship. The uniqueness of people's sovereignty is not lost, only it expresses itself both through the States governments and through the federal government.

As James Wilson argued in the Ratifying Convention of Pennsylvania, "the supreme power . . . resides in the PEOPLE, as the fountain of government . . . They can delegate it in such proportions . . . as they think proper . . . to the governments" and "to the government of the United States" (McMaster J.B. and Stone F., 316 and 302).

If, lastly, we take into consideration the Constitution's amending procedure, that is, the procedure by which the constituent power is exercised, one comes to the same conclusion. In fact, the power of constitutional revision is not attributed to any specific constitutional body. If such a solution had been adopted, the federal balance could have been exposed to the risk of being broken to the advantage of one of the two government levels constituting the Federation. Instead, the revision of the Constitution cannot depend on an initiative or a unilateral decision of the federal government, nor on one of the federated states, but only on their cooperation. The procedure always followed so far, out of the two provided for in the Constitution, requires a vote by the two branches of Congress with a two-thirds majority, followed by the ratification with a simple-majority vote by three-quarters of the states' legislative assemblies.

This means that the power of constitutional revision has been granted to the federal government and the federated states as a whole, so that it cannot be exercised without an agreement between those two powers. In conclusion, we can state that the constituent power in a federal state belongs in its indivisible unity to the people, which exercises it through a decision in which the legislative powers of both the federal government and the states participate.

In sum, in a Federation the juridical order is one, even if there is a plurality of legislative bodies. And there is one sovereignty, that of the Federation, that is exercised through a plurality of governments: the states' and the federal one. Thus, sovereignty belongs to the federal people, that exercises it through several power centres.

In *The Federalist* there is not an in-depth discussion about the value and the foundations of democracy. The contribution of this book to the theory of democracy has to do, instead, with the definition of a typology of forms of democratic government and the means for compounding democratic government with liberty. As to the typology of forms of democratic government, *The Federalist* differentiates between democracy, republic and federation.

Madison differentiates between democracy and a republic. "In a democracy, the people meet and exercise the government in person" (*The Federalist No.14*); but in the democracies of ancient Greece, although the popular assembly had deliberating powers, "many of the executive functions were performed not by the people themselves, but by officers elected by the people, and representing the people in their executive capacity" (*The Federalist No.63*). Thus, those democracies had some forms of representation. It is not appropriate to define them as forms of *direct democracy*. A more adequate name could be *assembly democracy*. By this expression we want to emphasize the central role the citizens' assembly had, and also that direct democracy is a myth which neglects the fact that human societies require political reflection and political mediation, or, to use Rousseau's language, that the general will cannot immediately coincide with the sum of particular wills.

Instead, in a republic the people "assemble and administer [the government] by their representatives and agents" (*The Federalist No.14*). It is the form of government that in contemporary language is defined *representative democracy*. Hence

> A democracy [. . .] will be confined to a small spot. A republic may be extended over a large region. As the natural limit of a democracy is that distance from the central point which will just permit the most remote citizens to assemble as often as their public functions demand, [. . .] so the natural limit of a republic is that distance from the centre which will barely allow the representatives to meet as often as may be necessary for the administration of public affairs (*The Federalist No.14*).

Also the *federal democracy* is a form of representative democracy, but constitutes an institutional innovation, as it doubles the democratic representation and is a different form of democratic government. Hamilton places the federal principle in the evolutionary process of republican institutions:

> The science of politics, however, like most other sciences, has received great improvement. The efficacy of various principles is now well understood, which

were either not known at all, or imperfectly known to the ancients. The regular distribution of power into distinct departments; the introduction of legislative balances and checks; the institution of courts composed of judges holding their offices during good behaviour; the representation of the people in the legislature by deputies of their own election: these are wholly new discoveries, or have made their principal progress towards perfection in modern times. They are means, and powerful means, by which the excellences of republican government may be retained and its imperfections lessened or avoided. To this catalogue of circumstances that tend to the amelioration of popular systems of civil government, I shall venture, however novel it may appear to some, to add one more: [. . .] I mean the ENLARGEMENT of the ORBIT within which such systems are to revolve, either in respect to the dimensions of a single state or to the consolidation of several smaller states into one great Confederacy" (*The Federalist No.9*).

Hamilton tries to identify which institutions made humankind progress towards good government. It is a very short list, which comprises division of powers, bicameralism, independence of the judiciary and people's representation in the legislative bodies. It shows that the invention of new institutions is a rare event in history. To this list he "ventures to add" the federal principle, "however novel it may appear", and defines it "the enlargement of the orbit" on which the "popular systems of civil government" revolve.

Only with the Constitution of the United States does the history of federalism begin. The preamble of the US Constitution starts with the words: "We the People of the United States [. . .] do ordain and establish this Constitution for the United States of America." The meaning of such words is clear. They mark the beginning of a new democratic era in the history of international organizations. With the Constitution of the United States a Union of states was formed which had no precedent in history: its constitutional bodies have a democratic, not a diplomatic structure.

While the government bodies of the Unions of States were formed until then by the representatives of the States and their decisions were applied to states, with the American Constitution they are directly elected by the people and their decisions are directly applied to citizens. The Federation is then a state, but does not possess all the features that states were having until then: the unification of all powers in one single centre. The federal institutions allow representative democracy to express itself on two (but potentially more than two) government levels. The federal system allows the self-government principle to be applied to a plurality of power centres, which coexist within a constitutional democratic framework that includes all of them.

This typology of forms of democratic government (assembly, representative and federal) points out the relationship between these three institutional innovations and the extension of a democratic state. With assembly-democracy the expansion of the dimension of the democratic state could not be greater than a city, i.e. the number of people that could gather in a square. Representative democracy made it possible to extend a democratic government to a national scale. Federal democracy has made it possible to form a democratic government of dimensions enclosing an entire region of the world, that potentially may be enlarged to the whole world (through the extension of the number of levels of democratic government).

The constitutional principle which the federal state is founded on is the plurality of power centres, coordinated with each other in such a way that to the federal government, with authority over the whole territory of the federation, a minimal amount of powers is granted, as necessary to ensure political and economic unity, and to the federated states, each of them with authority over its own territory, the residual powers are granted. Granting to the federal government the monopoly of competences over foreign and military policy makes it possible to eliminate the military frontiers between states, so that the relations among the states lose their violent character and take on a legal character, and every conflict can be settled in courts. Transferring to the federal institutions some competences in the economic field has the aim to eliminate the obstacles of customs and monetary nature which hinder the markets' unification, and give the federal government an autonomous decision-making authority in the field of economic policy. The consequence of this distribution of competences among a plurality of independent and coordinated power centres is that every part of the territory and every individual is subject to the authority of the federal government and to that of a federated state, without renouncing the principle of having only one decision-making site for every problem. Thus, the federal government, contrary to the unitary national state—which tends to homogenize all of the natural communities living on its territory, trying to impose on all citizens the same language and the same customs—, has very limited powers, because the federated states are provided with sufficient powers to autonomously rule themselves.

Such a balance between two orders of power possessing a democratic base makes the people, according to Hamilton, "master of its own destiny."

Power being almost always the rival of power, the general government will at all times stand ready to check the usurpations of the state governments, and these will have the same disposition towards the general government. The people, by throwing themselves into either scale, will infallibly make it preponderate. If their rights are invaded by either, they can make use of the other as the instrument of redress (*The Federalist No.28*).

Thus, the institutions typical of the centralizing states (the permanent armies based on compulsory conscription, the state schools, the great public rituals, the imposing on every smaller territorial community of the same administrative and prefectural guardianship-system) have never been experienced, and in any case have never taken root, in states with a federal or a highly decentralized regime. The federal structures, that do not require that the competence of school education be conferred to the central government (which also controls the army), to escape the tendency to totalitarian logic of the national states, which use their power to transform their citizens into good soldiers.

The federal constitutional balance, which lets the unity of the federation be compounded with the independence of its parts, is reflected in the composition of the legislative power, a branch of which represents the people of the federation in proportion to the number of voters, while the other branch is elected by the people of each member state with an equal number of representatives per state, independently of the differences in population. Laws must obtain the consent of the majority of the people's representatives and of the majority of the States.

In the United States, the executive power is entrusted to a single person, the President, who appoints the ministers, who are answerable to him. He exercises the powers of Head of State and Head of Government, is answerable for his actions not to the legislative power, but to the people, who elect him and may confirm or revoke their confidence every four years. Strength and stability allow the government to perform with efficacy a re-equilibrating function of social life and to carry out in an organic and coherent fashion the government program, while the bestowal of autonomous powers on the federated states constitutes the most efficient check to any abuse of power by the central government, and the most solid guarantee against the risk of dictatorship.

According to Hamilton, "energy in the Executive is a leading character in the definition of good government. [. . .] A feeble executive implies a feeble execution of the government. A feeble execution is but another phrase for a bad execution" (*The Federalist No. 70*). There is a tight correlation between concentration of power in the hands of one person and the strength of the executive: when the responsibility of the executive is given to more persons, "there is always danger of difference of opinion", which "might impede or frustrate the most important measures of the government, in the most critical emergencies of the state." Moreover, a plurality of persons running the executive power "tends to conceal faults and destroy responsibility", which "is shifted from one to another with so much dexterity, and under such plausible appearances, that the public opinion is left in suspense about the real author."

As a consequence, "the restraints of public opinion" over the government course "lose their efficacy" (*The Federalist No. 70*).

Finally, staying in office for a certain period of time constitutes the best guarantee for government stability. These considerations find a resounding confirmation *a contrario* in the feebleness, inefficiency, instability and irresponsibility of the parliamentary and multi-party systems in the European continent, which express multi-party coalition governments that can make and unmake governments depending on short-term considerations of theirs, and are unable to compound the need to strengthen the powers of the executive, arising from the growing number of areas requiring its intervention in the economic and social fields, with the preservation of free and democratic institutions.

On the other hand, there is to consider that in a presidential system the power organization is based on the separation between government and parliament, both elected, separately, by the people. The US constitutional experience has clearly shown that the legislative and the executive often express different and diverging political lines, and that the antagonism of the two powers has exposed government action to the danger of paralysis. The danger has become more serious in the 20th century, when the planning role of the state has become important. With regard to planning, that in an industrial society tends to absorb all of the government functions, a parliamentary system seems more suitable. In fact, it allows the prevalent trends among the people to be more efficiently asserted in front of the government, and at the same time it ensures a concerted action and thus coordination and unity of the political course among the various bodies of the state.

As far as the government's stability and efficiency requirements are concerned, there is to note that the British and the German parliamentary systems, thanks to the bi-polar party system (which is, conditions being equal, the result of political and institutional choices, for example an electoral system that eliminates the smaller parties, and a political decentralization that gives to new expectations emerging in society a better possibility to express themselves), have succeeded in getting the same result as the presidential systems: the direct election of the Head of government.

The federal model realizes a division of powers on a territorial basis, and such a constitutional balance cannot hold without the primacy of the Constitution over any other power. However, this does not imply the prevalence of the judiciary over other state powers. Hamilton notes, in fact:

> The judiciary, on the contrary, has no influence over either the sword or the purse [. . .] It is beyond comparison the weakest of the three departments of power; it can never attack with success either of the other two. [. . .] It is far

more rational to suppose that the courts were designed to be an intermediate body between the people and the legislature, in order, among other things, to keep the latter within the limits assigned to their authority. The interpretation of the laws is the proper and peculiar province of the courts. [. . .] If there should happen to be an irreconcilable variance between the two, that which has the superior obligation and validity ought, of course, to be preferred; or, in other words, the Constitution ought to be preferred to the statute, the intention of the people to the intention of their agents. Nor does this conclusion by any means suppose a superiority of the judicial to the legislative power. It only supposes that the power of the people is superior to both; and that where the will of the legislature, declared in its statutes, stands in opposition to that of the people, declared in the Constitution, the judges ought to be governed by the latter rather than the former. (*The Federalist No. 78*)

The peculiar feature of the federalist model is that in case of conflict the authority to decide in real terms what are limits that the two power orders cannot trespass is neither the central government (as happens in the unitary state, where the smaller territorial communities have only a delegated autonomy) nor the federated states (as happens in the confederal systems, which do not limit the absolute sovereignty of member states). Such power is granted to a neutral authority, the courts, which have the power of interpretation and constitutional revision of laws.

The constitutional history of the US has shown how the autonomy of the judiciary power is based on the balance between the central power and the peripheral powers, and how the courts have been able to efficiently fulfil their functions until the tendency to centralization of power, which began at the time of the world wars and gained strength in particular after World War Two, did not change the federal balance. But as long as that balance was maintained, to give strength to the rulings in constitutional matters have been now the federated states, now the central government, which have supported the rulings whenever they were converging with their respective interests. Hence, only by virtue of the decisions of the judiciary power can the balance between powers defined in the Constitution be re-established, whilst in the unitary State, where there is no autonomous power centre except the central government (which controls through the prefects the local bodies and is *de facto* the arbiter of the Constitution), and where the legislative and the executive inevitably tend to be controlled by the same political forces, the judiciary power and the Constitutional Courts are almost reduced to bodies of the public administration. In sum, whereas in the unitary democratic state there remains a residue of absolutism, because who makes the laws is not subject to the laws, in a federation, thanks to the coexistence and the competition of two orders of democratic governments and to the fact that the power to decide on the division of powers is awarded to the courts, the principles of the rule of law find their full realization.

The distribution of power on a territorial basis is actually much more efficient than that on a functional basis in assuring a divided control of power that is the main guarantee of political liberty, because both the federal government and the member states can found their independence on a different social base. On this matter, Hamilton argues that the federal system allows it to "reconcile the advantages of monarchy with those of republicanism" (*The Federalist No. 9*). In the cultural horizon of the theory of the unitary state, the contradiction between the requirement of political freedom, which can only be fulfilled in a small state, and that of military efficacy, which allows great monarchies to be strong and independent, is insurmountable. History presents countless examples of small states that have lost their liberty because they did not have the means to defend it, or that in the endeavour to enhance security had to sacrifice their liberty. Now, the federal system, thanks to its doubling of democratic representation, allows to reconcile the advantages of small dimensions—in which citizens have more possibilities to participate directly and with continuity in making political decisions and where power may be subject to a more direct control by the people, so that in local communities sufficient room can be given to self-government—with the advantages of large dimensions, as required by the modern conditions of industrial production and military techniques, and also necessary to assure economic development and political independence.

1.3. THE THEORY OF INTERNATIONAL RELATIONS

The theory of the federal state, being a theory of the supranational democratic governance—a government capable of controlling international relations and of subordinating the individual, particular *raisons d'état* of the states belonging to the same political system to the general interest of their federal union— constitutes an especially suitable view-point for arriving at a better comprehension of international politics. American federalism, mostly in the version of its highest theoretical conscience, that is Hamilton's, places itself in the tradition thinking of the theory of *raison d'état*. However, the authors who follow the theory of the power-State, from Georg Wilhelm Friedrich Hegel (1770–1831) to Leopold von Ranke (1795–1886) to Friedrich Meinecke (1862–1954), give to the theory of *raison d'état* a strong ideological character in a conservative and nationalist sense, so much so that the German ruling class founded on it the justification of Germany's authoritarianism and imperialism. Whereas in their conception the division of humankind in sovereign states, their rivalry, international anarchy, the violent character of the relations among states are natural and permanent features of historical reality, in federalist theoretical perspective such phenomena look as determined by history, and may therefore be overcome through a transformation of international relations.

The forming of the United States of America made it clear how the democratic structure of the thirteen states, which had gained their independence with the revolution, was not sufficient to ensure peace. The confederal link they had associated with one another, as it was not limiting the states' power, did not eliminate the use of force among them, or the threat to resort to it. It was the formation of a federal government that allowed them to replace force with law in the relations among them.

The Federalist outlines the fundamental features of an empirical theory of international politics. It is founded on a rigorous distinction between two configurations a system of sovereign states may take: international anarchy or a federal order; and it illustrates the qualitative leap that international relations take when a system of states is regulated by a higher power able to transform the force relations into juridical relations, and subject them to democratic control.

> A sovereignty over sovereigns,—one reads in *The Federalist*—a government over governments, a legislation for communities, as contradistinguished from individuals, as it is a solecism in theory, so in practice it is subversive of the order and ends of civil polity, by substituting violence in place of law, or the destructive coercion of the sword in place of the mild and salutary coercion of the magistracy. (*The Federalist No. 20*)

In the phenomenology of international relations, examined according to the theory of *raison d'état*, Hamilton rigorously drew the key discriminating line: the existence of a truly common power. This criterion allows us to single out the qualitative difference between federation and confederation. Whereas the first is a state, provided with a direct power over individuals and which individuals concur to form through democratic procedures, the second is not a state, but an international organization in which the states keep their absolute sovereignty and exert an exclusive power over individuals.

The decisions of the confederation's central body, based on the principle of the states' (not the citizens') equality, which assigns one vote to each state (not to each citizen) with no consideration given to the number of inhabitants, "contradict—as Hamilton wrote—that fundamental maxim of republican government, which requires that the sense of the majority should prevail" (*The Federalist No. 22*). In fact, confederations, basing themselves on the principle of the intangibility of states' sovereignty and excluding the people from the decisions regarding relations among states, have no procedures for taking decisions by majority voting. On important matters they decide by unanimous vote, with the result that a single member state can paralyse with its veto the entire confederation, such as "to subject the sense of the greater number to that of the lesser" (*The Federalist No. 22*). Forced, because of their structure, to suffer the dynamics of diverse and often diverging interests of the member states with no possibility to control it, and to reflect the contradictions that they, instead, should overcome, confederations are one variety of the wider category of alliances among states, from which they differ for the presence of a permanent body with a diplomatic status, instituted in order to settle the disputes among associated states and to arrive, if possible, at common decisions.

The distinction between federation and confederation illustrates, then, the radical difference that exists between a system of states in which a process of concentration of power has taken place, and a system of states in which every component still keeps the monopoly of force. Whereas in the first case the conflicts among states (and among political and social groups, and among individuals of different states) can be settled according to the law and in courts, in the second, in the absence of a mechanism for settling disputes at international level and due to the ensuing necessity for the states to protect themselves, the settling of conflicts will ultimately be left to force.

The experience of the US confederation and of the European system of powers had led Hamilton to formulate this principle: "To look for a continuation of harmony between a number of independent, unconnected sovereignties in the same neighbourhood, would be to disregard the uniform course of human events, and to set at defiance the accumulated experience of ages" (*The Federalist No. 6*). International anarchy is then the ground on which disputes among states may degenerate into wars. Consequently, in the federal conception, the fundamental cause for war lies in the absolute sovereignty of states, and only by overcoming international anarchy can people expect peace.

But Hamilton did not limit himself to formulate the principle that it is impossible to establish a peaceful order among sovereign states, unless they are subject to a higher power, but he also enunciated a very important corollary to the same: war is not caused, at least for what concerns the basic determining nexus, by the authoritarian nature of the states' political regime. The historical experience of republics shows that they have been involved in both offensive and defensive wars to the same extent as monarchies. So, according to Hamilton, it can be said that "There have been [. . .] almost as many popular as royal wars" (*The Federalist No. 6*).

That statement is very important for demystifying an ideological aspect of the liberal-democratic thought, whose followers were dreaming about a supposed peaceful spirit of the republics and were under the illusion that, once individual liberties were established and the control on government was put in people's hands, the war-leaning tendencies of states will die out.

It is true that democracies do not generally resort to war in order to solve the controversies that divide them, as the democratic peace theory maintains. But the lesson the followers of the theory draw from that empirical evidence—that the extension of democracy to non-democratic states is the main way that leads to peace—is dubious. Undoubtedly, the tendency of democracies towards peaceful behaviour lies in the structure of democratic government. In fact, democratic institutions hamper governments in resorting to violence in international relations. This restraint does not exist in those States where power is concentrated in a single constitutional organ (absolute monarchies, left or right-wing dictatorships, etc.). If it is true that liberal democracy is a brake on the aggressiveness of States, it is not an answer to the problem of international anarchy which has its root in the division of the world into sovereign States. In short, democracy can be defined as a necessary but insufficient condition for peace. Research into democracy has focused the national point of view, ignoring the fact that the progressive establishment of democracy at a national level has not been accompanied by democracy in relations between States. This limitation emphasizes the partial character of only establishing democracy at national level.

There is a fundamental difference between federalism and the other currents of modern political thought, including socialism and communism, which conceive peace as an automatic and necessary consequence of the transformation of the state's internal structures in a liberal, democratic, socialist or some other sense. The basic difference concerns the evaluation of international politics, of peace and war. In federalist theory, power politics, imperialism and war are not ascribed to the authoritarian structure of government or to the capitalist mode of production, but essentially to international anarchy, that is to say, to the mere division of humankind in sovereign states, as a consequence of which every state, whatever its political regime and production system, must yield to the law of force to protect its independence.

But the exposition of Hamilton's theory of international relations is still too generic, unless we introduce a further description of the concept of international anarchy. In fact, the anarchy situation in which international relations are embedded does not produce the same consequences on every state. The extent to which states are involved in their struggle with other states depends largely on the position they occupy in a given system of states. The role that a system of states assigns to each state conditions both its foreign policy and its internal policy and even its constitutional arrangement. Hamilton differentiates between insular-type and continental-type states. While the first, thanks to the natural defences they are provided with, are little exposed to the danger of invasion and hence have a more peaceful foreign policy, the second, subject to a constant political and military pressure at their borders, are more exposed to the impact of international disputes and, therefore, their foreign policy is more belligerent. Also their internal policy and their very state structure tend to conform to the foreign policy tasks imposed by the state's position in the international political system. Thus, according to Hamilton,

> Safety from external danger is the most powerful director of national conduct. Even the ardent love of liberty will, after a time, give way to its dictates. The violent destruction of life and property incident to war, the continual effort and alarm attendant on a state of continual danger, will compel nations the most attached to liberty to resort for repose and security to institutions which have a tendency to destroy their civil and political rights. To be more safe, they at length become willing to run the risk of being less free. (*The Federalist No. 8*)

The state, forced to concentrate more on the problems of defence, must set up large permanent armies and, in order to quickly get the army mobilized and to take decisions rapidly, which is vital to counter external dangers, will be pushed "to strengthen the executive arm of government, in doing which their constitutions would acquire a progressive direction toward monarchy. It is of the nature of war to increase the executive at the expense of the legislative authority." (*The Federalist No. 8*)

The traditional political thinking neglects the influence that international relations exercise on the structures of States. Consequently it does not take into account that, even though democracies do not wage war with other democracies, the search for security often leads governments to sacrifice democracy.

The last stage of the political power-concentration process will be the prevailing of the military over the civil power. In the continental-type state,

> The continual necessity for their services enhances the importance of the soldier, and proportionally degrades the condition of the citizen. The military state becomes elevated above the civil. The inhabitants of territories, often the theatre of war, are unavoidably subjected to frequent infringements on their rights, which serve to weaken their sense of those rights; and by degrees the people are brought to consider the soldiery not only as their protectors, but as their superiors. The transition from this disposition to that of considering them masters, is neither remote nor difficult. (*The Federalist No. 8*)

On the other hand, the insular-type states, having no borders in common with other states, are little influenced by the logic of power in international relations, and leave more room to the factors that favour the free development of society. To illustrate the advantages of the insular position, Hamilton describes the situation of Great Britain and compares it with that of the states of the continent:

> An insular situation, and a powerful marine, guarding it in a great measure against the possibility of foreign invasion, supersede the necessity of a numerous army within the kingdom [. . .] This peculiar felicity of situation has, in a great degree, contributed to preserve the liberty which that country to this day enjoys, in spite of the prevalent venality and corruption. If, on the contrary, Britain had been situated on the continent, and had been compelled, as she would have been, by that situation, to make her military establishments at home coextensive with those of the other great powers of Europe, she, like them, would in all probability be, at this day, a victim to the absolute power of a single man. (*The Federalist No. 8*)

The theory of *raison d'état* allowed Hamilton not only to shed light on the mechanism that has governed the policy and history of the European system of states, but also to forecast the historical evolution of the United States' institutions.

> If we should be disunited, and the integral parts should either remain separated, or, which is most probable, should be thrown together into two or three confederacies, we should be, in a short course of time, in the predicament of the continental powers of Europe—our liberties would be a prey to the means of defending ourselves against the ambition and jealousy of each other (*The Federalist No. 8*).

Should the United States have been forced to concentrate on the necessity of defending itself, it would have had an authoritarian evolution, building up a large permanent army and concentrating power in the executive. But America could have escaped such destiny:

> If we are wise enough to preserve the Union, we may for ages enjoy an advantage similar to that of an insulated situation. Europe is at a great distance from us. [. . .] Extensive military establishments cannot, in this position, be necessary to our security" (*The Federalist No. 8*).

Only a "powerful marine" would be sufficient to defend America.

The North-American constitutional experience has drawn attention to the first ideas of a federalist political thought (the fundamental lines of the theory of the federal state and of the theory of international relations), but also to the limits of a purely institutional conception of federalism. In fact, American federalism was not an independent political experience. Its historical relevance consists in its novel form of power organization, brought about by the federal Constitution. It was conceived by its founders as an instrument to consolidate the liberal-democratic values in the North-American society, and had no intention to create new ones. What makes Hamilton's thought different is its peculiar evaluation of the dangers the free institutions are exposed to because of international anarchy, and his idea of North-America's federal unification as a means to gain political insularity. On the other hand, the US federal Constitution is more the result of fortunate historical circumstances, which have shielded its liberal-democratic institutions from conflicts among classes and among states, than of the intention to experiment a new model of political life. It was established in a part of the world where the threat of harsh social tensions was held in check by the possibility offered to oppressed people to settle in vast open spaces, and where isolationism, made possible by political unification, has protected the United States from the centralizing effects that international conflicts could have had. American federalism can be considered therefore as a subordinate political concept to liberalism and democracy.

Chapter Two

Kant, World Federation, Perpetual Peace, and Human Emancipation

Considering the Constitution of the United States of America, one cannot but conclude that it does introduce a new instrument of political organization of society, whose universal goal is perpetual peace. But neither in *The Federalist Papers* nor in any other contemporary work on a similar subject, as usual for the pragmatic nature of the Anglo-Saxon culture, can any consideration be found on a possible global significance of this new institutional instrument. It was presented more as a means for solving the political problems of Americans than as a model of democratic government of international organizations. Universal peace and cosmopolitanism were possible options only on the plane of reason, not on that of political struggle. In sum, the founding fathers conceived the Constitution of the United States as a means for ensuring peace and liberty to Americans through their isolationism.

In the political, juridical, philosophical and historical writings of Immanuel Kant (1724–1804) we find the first formulation of some essential elements of the federalist theory, considered as a political project having a global character. What is peculiar to Kant's conception of federalism is, on the one hand, the negation of war and international anarchy, denounced as the main factors that cripple man and prevent his free development, and, on the other, the recognition of an indissoluble connection between world federation, perpetual peace and human emancipation.

Kant's project of perpetual peace (1795), worked out during the French Revolution, at the dawn of the era of nationalism, is profoundly different from those of the thinkers before him, because it is not conceived of as a proposal to be presented to governments or diplomats for reaching a better balance of power among states. Challenging the idea that international law and the balance of power are efficient means for ensuring peace, he formulates a belief that the history of divisions and wars in the Europe of nation-states will confirm. Arguing that only federalism allows for peace to be established, he defines its value in completely new terms, namely as the expression of the necessity to unify the peoples, which had come onto the stage of history with the French Revolution, and to create a supranational democratic government.

Kant considers peace as the goal of the course of history: "From the throne of its moral legislative power, reason absolutely condemns war as a means of determining the right, and makes seeking the state of peace a matter of unmitigated duty" (Kant I., 1988, 116). However, history displays a dialectical nature: reason makes its way through by labouring in a tortuous way, along which conflicts, violence, wars are as many vehicles that allow reason to assert itself. Kant considers antagonism the springboard of success: "men's *unsocial sociability*, i.e., their tendency to enter into society, combined, however with a thoroughgoing resistance that constantly threatens to sunder this society" (Kant I., 1988, 31–32). On the one hand, reason develops in man "a propensity for *living in society*, for in that state he feels himself to be more than man. i.e., feels himself to be more than the development of his natural capacities" (Kant I., 1988, 32). On the other, "he also has [. . .] a great tendency to isolate himself, for he finds in himself the unsociable characteristic of wanting everything to go according to his own desires" (Kant I., 1988, 32). His instinct, which arouses antagonism among individuals and seems to hinder any social progress, constitutes instead the indispensable stimulus to societal development, at least up to that era in history when reason will have fully asserted itself.

According to Kant, history is the territory of reason's gradual assertion; reason, since its first manifestation, imposes to treat other men as ends, not means, on the basis of the principle of "*equality of all rational beings*" (Kant I., 1988, 53). This means that, as gradually as reason frees man from the law of nature, liberty and equality develop and grows man's ability to control the course of history. On the other hand, the man who negates his fellow's reason does not only negate reason, but also the principles of liberty and equality. Therefore it is impossible that a single individual may behave in a rational manner, if all other individuals do not behave in a rational manner. Building a rational society is the ultimate objective history is tending to; it proceeds in a dialectical way through obstacles and difficulties that sometimes stop reason's progress and even cause a regression, and yet they are the springboard for further progress. The course of history allows us to appreciate the role of reason as the force transforming society; it subjects the established order to a constant strain in order to conform the world of politics to the order of reason.

However, the imperative of practical reason is not sufficient by itself to ensure that the principles of liberty and equality are realized. There have to be the rule of law and a juridical order that assure their application. As long as it is not guaranteed that nobody is allowed to use force against other people, through the institution of a juridical order to which all individuals subject themselves, everyone's security is threatened by his mere proximity to another individual, even if he is not actually hurting anybody. In the absence of a common spot people can turn to, i.e. a law giving the possibility to peacefully settle the disputes among individuals, everybody would have to permanently stand alert and armed, presuming to have to take the law into his own hands.

For Kant, historical progress materializes by organizing society according to a rational law, that allows individuals to abandon the state of nature, and transform force relations into law relations. The first stage of this route is represented by the formation of the state, which, to use a Weber-derived formula, takes in its hands the monopoly of force, making peaceful coexistence among individuals possible. This is not the outcome of an impulse driving men to a spontaneous cooperation, convenient for satisfying their needs, but is the consequence of the coercion by the state, which lets individual whims be subjected to law. So, the progressive humanization of power will not eliminate coercion, but will replace the coercion exerted by narrow groups with self-coercion of everybody towards everybody, so that the state becomes the expression of a general will that allows everybody to be free and equal.

However, the use of force (or the threat to resort to force) continues to be the normal instrument in international political life, even in the relations among states that have eliminated from their internal structures the most censurable political and social inequalities. The wicked part of human nature, which is restrained by the coercion exerted by the state, reveals itself with no limits in international relations. Actually, international anarchy is the situation that forces the states to defend their independence with arms. Hence, international relations still belong with the pre-juridical sphere of the state of nature.

Therefore, Kant defines "a mere figment of imagination" the idea of a stable universal peace established on the basis of the balance of power. He compares it with that Swift's house, "whose architect built it so perfectly in accord with all the laws of equilibrium, that as soon as a sparrow lit on it, it fell in" (Kant I., 1988, 89). Nor is international law—which modern international organizations like the League of Nations or the UN, having no power of their own, have to conform to—an efficient instrument for eliminating war. In fact, every state cannot but count on force to ensure its security and protect its rights. It "presupposes the existence of many *separate*, independent, adjoining nations; and although such a situation is in itself a state of war" (Kant I., 1988, 124–125). The battlefield is indeed the court where as the last resort the conflicts among states are decided, but a victory conquered by the force of

arms, Kant wrote, "cannot determine the right" (Kant I., 1988,116). Ultimately, international law, being a "right to go to war" (Kant I., 1988,117), is
not worth the name of law. Thomas Hobbes (1588–1679) wrote in the
Leviathan that "where there is no common power, there is no law" (Hobbes
T., 85) and that "the end of this institution [the state] is the peace" (Hobbes
T., 123). These fundamental statements give a precise indication about the relations between State, right and peace.

In tune with that viewpoint, Kant believes that the state is the great peace-
maker between human groups. However, his project of juridical pacifism
goes beyond Hobbes' in three directions, as made clear in the "three definitive articles" of an imaginary treaty for "perpetual peace among nations"
(Kant I., 1998, 111). In the first place, through the transformation of all absolute governments in republican governments: "The civil constitution of
every nation should be republican" (Kant I., 1988, 112). Secondly, Kant
hopes that sates give up their "lawless freedom" and unite in a "universal republic" which should extend "to include all the people of the earth" (Kant I.,
1988, 117), so that international law "shall be based on a federation of free
states" (Kant I., 1988, 115). In fact, a state conforms to the idea it embodies
only if it eliminates all force relations from political life. Thirdly, by overcoming the dichotomy between "civil rights of men in a nation" and "the
rights of nations" at international level, and establishing "the rights of world
citizenship so far as men and nations stand in mutually influential relations as
citizens of a universal nation of men (*ius cosmopoliticum*)" (Kant I., 1988,
112). The world federation is the community which does not exclude anybody, which does not have the notion of foreigner.

The state, which is the vehicle of peace inside its borders, is at the same
time the vehicle of war in the relations among states. Therefore humanity is
"no more than halfway" (Kant I., 1988, 36) in its development. As the concentration of force in state's hands is the condition for progressively arriving
at a situation (the republican government) where the use of force, even by the
state, is brought to a minimum or even made not necessary by the growing
adaptation of individual behaviour to the principles of reason, likewise the
world federation represents the second and final stage in the struggle for oust-
ing violence from political life and creating the conditions for a rational and
democratic solution to all social conflicts. The universal federation is then the
necessary final answer to the urge that drives men to associate themselves in
society.

Most Kant's interpreters (for example Norberto Bobbio (1999, 485–486),
Jürgen Habermas (1998, 166–171) and David Held (1995, 226–231)) believe
that his fear of a universal despotism, which could constitute the outcome of
the evolution of a state of world dimensions, has driven him to opt for the

world federation's "negative surrogate" (Kant I., 1998, 117), that is, the world confederation. Instead, Kant rejects both a *"universal monarchy"*, which could lead "to the most terrifying despotism" (Kant I., 1988, 88), and a *confederation* or league of sovereign States, which would not be capable of "putting an end to war." Both solutions would be contrary to the goal of perpetual peace, as Giuliano Marini (1998) has shown quite convincingly. The alternative to the "universal monarchy" is the "world republic", and the alternative to the confederation is the federation, which in one of his most precise formulations is defined "Völkerbund als Weltrepublik", i.e. a republic of confederated free peoples (Kant I., 1914, 34). As Mario Albertini has noted, in Kant's time

> nobody, except Hamilton in part, really knew what a federal State is. This difficulty, of course, was present in Kant also and it is true that he did not overcome it. But it is also true that every time he poses the problem of peace he always thinks of a world power that is able to impose the observance of a universal law, although when he attempts to define the nature of such a power, he is not able do it, like every man of his time (Albertini, M., 1985, 15).

Consistently with such premises, Kant defines peace as the organization that does not seek "merely to stop *one* war", but "seeks to end *all* wars forever" (Kant I., 1988, 117). Peace is not just the absence of hostilities, or "the suspension of hostilities" in the interval between two wars (negative peace). "The state of peace [is not] a natural state", but is something that "must be *established*" (Kant I., 1988, 111) through the creation of a legal order guaranteed by a power above the states (positive peace). Defining peace as the political organization that makes war impossible, Kant has rigorously indicated the line separating peace from war, and has placed truce (that is the situation where, even if hostilities have ceased, the threat remains that they may resume) in the same category as war.

For Kant the essential condition for peace is law, or more precisely the extension of law to all of social relations, in particular to the sphere of international relations. Only within a universal federation of free peoples will international right become a full-fledged juridical reality, founded on a power able to regulate relations among states and to prevent men, isolated or in groups, from resorting to violence for settling their disputes. Thus, the idea of a world federation, which ensures perpetual peace, represents Kant's final crowning to his theory of law, politics and philosophy of history, and not just a marginal aspect of his thought, as proven by the fact that he makes reference to it in all of his major works.

However, Kant believes that "at the stage of culture at which the human race still stands, war is an indispensable means for bringing it to a still higher stage" (Kant I., 1988, 58). In fact, the fear of war represents the only effective defence of human rights against authoritarian and oppressive governments. Historical experience confirms that resorting to violence has usually been the tool for bringing about liberty and equality. It is evident that as long as there will be arbitrary governments with no constitutional limits or founding themselves on discrimination and class exploitation, which can only be defeated by resorting to violence (or threatening to do so), peace is the synonym of conservation of authoritarian and unjust orders. This explains why in the liberal, democratic and socialist ideologies, which still provide the basic criteria for political thought and action, violence does not represent a solution to be rejected *a priori*, because it may play a progressive role, and peace is not considered a priority objective. Instead, pre-eminence has been given to the values of liberty, equality and social justice, which are pursued, if necessary, even with war. They represent the prerequisite for any initiative aiming at bringing about peace. If those principles are not well-established, it is not possible to put in place any form of civil coexistence based on peaceful relations among individuals, in other words: social peace. On the other hand, the choice to join the Federation must be free (this differentiates a Federation from an empire). For these reasons Kant argues that peace becomes possible only if the states joining the Federation have a republican Constitution, i.e. a form of political organization where everybody abides by a law wanted by all and protecting the community of free and equal men. In fact, in such a Constitution everybody accepts some limits to the exercise of his own liberty, subjecting himself to a common law equal for all and which everybody is willing to obey, because everybody has contributed to draft it.

Also the assumption of the democratic systems' supposed peaceful character has been proved patently wrong in the epoch of nationalism. History has shown that liberal-democratic institutions constitute a restraint on the state's aggressiveness in the international plane, and that the democratic states, at least in their reciprocal relations, follow a less bellicose line of conduct. However, the fact remains that the republican system cannot reach perfection as long as the world is divided in independent and sovereign states conflicting with each other. On this subject Kant incisively writes: "The problem of establishing a perfect civil Constitution depends on the problem of law-governed external relations among nations, and cannot be solved unless the latter is" (Kant I., 1988, 34). The investment of a great part of productive resources in armaments, the continuing military training every state is compelled to by the political division of mankind, the periodical ravages caused by war constitute a permanent obstacle to social development and humanization of political life.

As a consequence, the state's need of security and power tends by necessity to prevail over that of liberty for individuals and autonomy for the communities where they live, transforming men into "machines and tools in the hands of another"—the state—and turning upside down the relation between ends and means proclaimed by the Christian religion and by the liberal, democratic and socialist political thought. And this—Kant wrote—"is inconsistent with the rights of humanity." (Kant I., 1998, 108). In fact, every state bases its independence on the army and on its power to oblige every citizen to kill and die for his fatherland. And such a power can legitimise itself only on the condition that the state mystifies in the individuals' conscience the universal nature of the Christian, liberal, democratic and socialist values, and extorts from his citizens an exclusive loyalty, with the ensuing consequence to sacrifice and subordinate loyalty to humankind to that to one's fatherland.

That is why Kant qualifies war as the greatest obstacle to morality. Since all individuals are forced to conform their behaviour to a social structure modelled on the state's authoritarian and war-leaning needs, and their conscience to the ethics of violence that such a structure generates, their abilities develop in a unilateral direction and their moral growth is limited. But all this is not inescapable. On the contrary, it is the direct consequence of the irrational way humankind is organized, of its political division, of the state of anarchy it is surrounded with.

For the first time Kant limpidly enunciates the basic principles of the federalist theory, which singles out international anarchy as the factor that prevents liberty, democracy and justice from consolidating within states, and indicates peace, i.e. the creation of an international juridical order, as the condition for defeating the war-leaning and authoritarian tendencies, always dormant in a state. It is an outright overturning of the point of view still prevalent in the liberal, democratic and socialist ideologies, dominated by the idea of giving priority to the state's reform from within, rather than to the goal of changing the international order, and by the illusion that peace is the automatic consequence of the establishment of liberal, democratic and socialist principles in the states. A precise and generally ignored criterion is identified, which explains not only the reason why the establishment of liberal, democratic and socialist principles did not coincide with the beginning of an era of peace, but also the partial and elusive nature of the establishment of those principles in a world of sovereign states conflicting with each other. Through Kant's thought, federalism distinguishes itself as the ideology that, for the first time in history, considers the value of peace to be the result of a specific struggle against the states' absolute sovereignty and in favour of a democratic world government.

Once liberty and equality are established everywhere with republican states and peace is established in the world federation, both the quality of social relations and the motives of individual life will undergo, according to Kant, a radical transformation. Once the power to keep within the bounds of law all social behaviours is acquired, the circle of *raisons d'état*, hence force relations in international politics, hence war, will be broken, and the legitimation of violence of man over man, coming from war and from permanently threatening war, will cease. Only at this stage in history will reason's struggle to subdue the resistance of nature and to eliminate force as a means for conflict resolution gain a final victory. Society will have acquired the power to self-rule in a rational manner, men will not be compelled in any circumstance to resort to force for getting moral goals, and their conduct could fully conform to the principle of the autonomy of will. As Kant wrote, "it is possible to make politics commensurable with morality only in a federative union" (Kant I., 1998, 138). This form of political organization implies a radical transformation of the relations between the individual and society, which will mark the attainment of the necessary conditions for the state's decline, for the trend to dissolving power in society and for realizing Kant's "kingdom of ends", in which it will be possible to treat men as ends in all social relations.

Kant is no utopian. He has carried out the analysis of the value of peace purely on the plane of reason, but he was aware that the imperative of reason would not be sufficient to persuade people to pursue that goal. Only the experience of the negativity of war, of the ravages and the misery it bedevils mankind with, of the continuous military preparations imposed by defence obligations, will drive the states, in an undefined future, to renounce their "lawless liberty" and yield to a common law and to a power that gives it strength. This should happen first in the states that will feel war's destructive violence as unbearable, so much as to persuade them to establish federal ties (most likely in Europe); and such a federal core should later extend itself to embrace all peoples on earth. His federalist theory is based therefore on a dialectical conception of history, which hinges on the contradictions of a world divided in states, governed by force relations, and arrives at last to a form of political organization of human kind founded on the rational and democratic control of world politics.

The importance of Kant's approach to peace lies in the identification of the main preliminary conditions that only now are bringing universal and permanent peace nearer. The first condition is represented by the experience of the devastation of war, which will have pushed nations "to give up the savage (lawless) freedom" (Kant I., 1998, 117). The events of the 20th century and in particular the destructive potential of the World Wars seem to have been the decisive factor that has driven Europe's (and in perspective the world's) governments to choose the route to peace. The second is the increase of exchanges, "since the earth is a globe", people would have to live "in close proximity" (Kant I., 1988, 118); the third is the states' institutional evolution, that should lead to the establishment of "a republican civil constitution" (Kant I., 1988, 112), founded on liberty and equality; the fourth is the shaping up of a world public opinion, since "a transgression of rights in *one* place of the world is felt *everywhere*" (Kant I., 1988, 119).

These conditions too appear to be materializing. On the one hand, the globalization process has upset the national states and has made clear the need of new power centres at the level of the great regions of the world and of the whole world. On the other, after the fall of the fascist and communist regimes, the majority of the UN member states are governed by representative democracy; this fact in turn constitutes the premise for extending that form of government to the relations among states, that is to say to experiment international democracy, which has found in the European Parliament its laboratory. Finally, thanks to communication technologies, every day we are informed about the events occurring in every part of the world. Because of this, a growing popular sensitivity is forming about world politics, so that one can rightly talk of the shaping up of a world public opinion and a global civil society. And this has repercussions on the evolution of international law, which tends to address itself no longer to States only, but to individuals too. Examples are the Universal Declaration of Human Rights (1948) and the institution of the permanent International Criminal Court (1998), which is empowered to indict and sentence individuals guilty of genocide, war crimes and crimes against humanity. This means that the premises are being created for overcoming the distinction between domestic and international law, and for the recognition of a cosmopolitan law.

The Kantian tradition, which remained dormant throughout the era of nationalism, is revived in the new phase of world history started with the end of Cold War. There are many scholars, e.g. Jürgen Habermas (1998), David Held (1995) and Otfried Höffe (1999), who maintain that Kant's vision of a World federal republic is an answer to the problems raised in the contemporary world by globalization and the erosion of state sovereignty.

The creation of new forms of statehood at world level seems to be the only alternative to the mastery of the market system and the spread of violence. The universal goals of the constitutionalization of international relations and international democracy provide the contemporary man with a guiding principle in the increasing confusion brought about by the process of globalization.

Thus, Kant is the first great federalist thinker, and his theoretical contribution is to have founded federalism on an autonomous vision of values and of the course of history. Kant correctly conceived a peaceful world order to be a legal order above the states, a conception which allowed him to give a rigorous definition of peace and to carry out a critique of international law and of the principle of balance of power valid forever.

Kant's philosophy of history and his idea of a world federation presuppose an awareness of the world's and humanity's tendency towards unification. As will be made clear later by Karl Marx (1818–1883), this process has its roots in the social transformations caused by the industrial revolution, i.e. in the horizontal increase of social relations, in the formation of a world-wide market and in the ever-growing interdependence of the societies composing mankind. Today, the process of social integration, that is extending people's material interdependence beyond the States' borders, and is producing "a universal intercourse between individuals" (as Marx and Engels (1820–1895) wrote in *German Ideology* (Marx K. Engels F., 2000, chapt. 1 § 5) "world-historical, empirical individuals in place of local ones"), is creating the social bases of cosmopolitanism.

However, the course of world history becomes accessible to a rational control and may be subject to the management of humankind on the condition that, side by side with that objective tendency, identified by Marxism, that drives the world towards an ever-stronger social integration, an action is carried out aiming at the political unification of mankind along the lines suggested by Kant, leading to a world federation. In fact, the objective tendency I have mentioned above does not necessarily lead to a world federation and to the elimination of violence from history, but only creates the conditions for achieving that goal.

Chapter Three

The Federalist Component
of the French Revolution

3.1 THE CONTRADICTION BETWEEN
NATIONALISM AND FEDERALISM

The federalist ideals were present in Europe during the French Revolution both in the aspiration to transform the state's internal structures by the decentralization of political power, and in the aspiration to overcome the divisions among states and to unify Europe and the world. While the first ideal found an expression in the Girondist faction, which was proposing to transform France in a federal system and institute the principles of self-government in local and regional communities, the idea of a community of free peoples, united in attaining peace, is common to all the factions of the French Revolution.

The feature of universality is intrinsic in the values that led to the fall of the *ancien régime*. With the Revolution there begins the process of liberating nations from the monarchic government, as a result of which they will eventually become the protagonists of international politics. The problem of the international order was posed in new terms and universal peace appeared as the result of the establishment of the principle of popular sovereignty worldwide. Here is how François-Constantin Chasseboeuf, called Volney (1757–1820), illustrates these ideas to the National Assembly in May 1790, in his famous peace declaration to the world:

You will not bear any longer that millions of men be the plaything of a few who are but the likes of them, and you will give back dignity and their rights to nations. The deliberation you are going to take today has such a significance, which marks the epoch of this great passage. Today you are making your entry into the political world. Till this moment you have deliberated in France and for

France; today you are going to deliberate for the universe and in the universe.
You are going to convene, I dare say, the assembly of nations (Lange C.L., 338).

Then Volney proposed a decree, which was not to be put to the vote, but
will be taken in its substance into the Constitution of 1791, about the French
nation renouncing the war of conquest. In it was stated that humankind constitutes a single society, whose goal is peace and happiness for all peoples;
that peoples enjoy the same natural rights the individuals do, and, consequently, no people has the right to invade the property of other peoples and to
deprive them of their freedom. However, as Hamilton had understood, the
democratic transformation of a state is never sufficient by itself to eliminate
the use of force from international relations. It is no surprise then that the revolutionary government decided, in its struggle with other states, to resort to
war. But even then the universalist thrust of the principles of 1789 did not
fade out. War will be seen as an instrument for freeing peoples from absolutism, thus creating the conditions for making universal peace possible.

Even in revolutionary France there was who, like Anacharsis Cloots
(1755–1794), a German nobleman living in France since 1776), warned that
unless the barriers that divide and put peoples one against the other were
eliminated, the principles of 1789 could not fully materialize and that it was
necessary therefore to extend to the international arena the principles of democratic government. The contemporaneous call for democracy and federalism
is not an exclusive feature of American history. With the French Revolution,
i.e. with its contemporaneous call for the democratic and the national principles, in Europe too the need was asserted to subject international policy to
popular control.

It was not just a purely ideal need, coming from the fact that reason pre-
cludes us from thinking that democracy is to be kept confined to one national
territory only. There was also an important practical problem, whose importance will be felt more and more with the progress of democratic and social
reforms in the states and with the parallel extension of the national principle:
the incompatibility between Europe's organization in national states and the
international order. This problem, which begun to appear in the French Revolution more in ideal than in practical terms, as a contradiction between the
rights of man and of the citizen on the national plane, and their negation on
the international plane, will never disappear from the underground current of
European history, because international relations have maintained their ten-
dentiously violent character. Thus, the federalist solution will always be present as one of the components of the revolutionary, democratic, socialist and
communist ideals, and will come to the surface every time Europe will be
shaken by crises serious enough to put forward fundamental political problems, like that of peace or liberty and justice at the international level.

They still were, to be sure, vague and inaccurate formulations (Cloots in 1793 thinks of "a unitary world republic" organized into one thousand departments on the model of the French republican system), which reflect the distance separating thought from the possibility to materialize it in practice, but which constitute indispensable orienting criteria in the face of the new contradictions and problems emerging in the course of history. In the European continent, unlike in the North American, the federalist ideals will be confronted with insurmountable obstacles. It was a matter of overcoming the divisions of historically consolidated states that, until 1945, will keep their international autonomy and will play a protagonist role in world politics, and not of unifying a system of small states situated at the margin of world politics, which had homogeneous features and just a few years of political independence.

As Mario Albertini (1919–1997) has pointed out, in the European continent two historical factors, namely class struggle (which has split the entire society in its midst, making the sense of belonging to one of the conflicting sides prevail over any other group-solidarity, and prevented the establishment of strong solidarity ties in local communities, indispensable for the emergence and the persistence of social bi-polarity, typical of a federal society), and power conflicts (which have led to the strengthening of central power, necessary for a swift mobilization of society in case of war, at the expense of local power), have prevented the establishment of federalism (Albertini M., 1993, 50–55). Instead, in the United States social tensions have been mitigated by the abundance of resources available in the boundless lands of the West. Hegel (1917, 199) considering this fact noted: "Were the German forests still in existence, the French Revolution would have not taken place." Moreover, the international conflicts have been contained thanks to the US political insularity and the British hegemony over the seas. The difficulty to find grouped together the political, historical and social conditions allowing the federal institutions to function explains the marginal character of federalism, which in the 19th century could establish itself only in peripheral areas of the world. In fact, federalism developed in areas where the centralizing pressure of international conflicts was weak, that is to say, in States which had chosen for themselves a neutral (Switzerland) or isolationist (the United States) role, and where class struggle took place in a mitigated fashion thanks to the possibility the oppressed were offered to colonize immense free spaces (and in fact federalism in the United States, Canada and Australia has many features in common with colonialism), or in a small State, like Switzerland, where government problems have an administrative, more than a political, character, that is to say, in situations where class struggle did not take so radical forms as to prevent the formation of some sort of solidarity within grass-root communities.

As Alexis de Tocqueville (1805–1859) has made clear, the Jacobin bureaucratic and military centralizing policy was necessary for domestic reasons (in order to defeat aristocracy, which was founding its power on local institutions organized according to principles of inequality and privilege, and to
destroy what was surviving of the feudal system), and for international reasons (in order to efficiently counter their bordering states in the tension-rid-
den atmosphere of the European continent). The supporters of federalism
ended up being taken for the defenders of feudal particularism and of the
privileges of the aristocratic classes, and for allies of the enemies of the Revolution.

It is to be mentioned that federalism became an accusation that brought
many people to the guillotine, among them the author of the French translation of *The Federalist*, Charles-Marie Trudaine de la Sablière (1792). Cloots'
tragedy shows in an exemplary way what costs the choice of cosmopolitism
was bringing with it. He was accused of being a member of the "party of the
strangers" and paid with the gallows his choice to qualify himself "citizen of
the world." Maximilien Robespierre (1758–1794) in 1793, when the Revolution entered the route of nationalist mobilization, in a speech that ended up
with Cloots' expulsion from the Jacobin Club, said:

> Can we consider a patriot a German baron? Citizens, let us be on our guard
> against the foreigners who want to be more patriotic than the French! Cloots,
> you spend your life with our enemies, with the agents and spies of foreign pow-
> ers; like them, you are a traitor we must look after [. . .] I accuse Cloots of hav-
> ing increased the number of the supporters of federalism. His extravagant ideas,
> his obstinacy in talking of a universal Republic [have a] seditious [character] [.
> . .] Paris is teeming with meddlers, Englishmen, Austrians. They are among us
> together with Frederic's agents [. . .] Cloots is a Prussian (Robespierre M.,
> 653–655).

The fact is that in a world of sovereign nations in conflict with each other,
in which every nation exacts an exclusive loyalty from its citizens, the choice
of cosmopolitism becomes treason of one's fatherland, which deserves to be
punished with the death sentence.

3.2 SAINT-SIMON AND THE PROJECT
TO REORGANIZE EUROPEAN SOCIETY

While the diplomats from all over Europe were meeting in the Congress of
Vienna for restoring on the ruins of the Napoleonic empire the old order based
on the principles of dynastic legitimacy and the balance of powers, Claude-

Henry de Saint-Simon (1760–1825) published in October 1814, together with Augustin Thierry (1795–1856), his booklet *On the Reorganization of European Society*. It reflects the new character the pacifist literature took after the American Revolution (which Saint-Simon had taken part in) and the French Revolution. In contrast with the political conception of the era of the Restoration, Saint-Simon argues that the conditions for international coexistence should be reconstructed on the basis of the democratic principle, and not trying to turn the wheel of history backwards.

On the one hand, he observes that "the balance of power is the most wrong arrangement one can make, because peace had to be its objective, and yet it has produced nothing but wars." On the other, he criticizes Saint-Pierre's project of perpetual peace, which entrusts to treaties among monarchs the realization of international order.

Can monarchs, who make treaties among themselves,—he asks himself—and plenipotentiaries, appointed by the contracting parties and removable by them, hold other views but partial ones and other interests but their own? (Saint-Simon C.-H. de, Thierry A., 175–177, vol. 1).

For bringing about peace in Europe it is necessary to abandon the old schemes of diplomacy.

The point of view I have placed myself in is that of the common interest of the European peoples—Saint-Simon writes. This is the only point of view where one can perceive both the evils threatening us and the means to avert those evils. Have those who are running public affairs rise to the same height and they will see what I have seen (Saint-Simon C.-H. de, Thierry A., 246, vol. 1).

Only by overcoming the difficulty consisting in the fact that the normal reference of political thought is one's own state and the one of political action is the struggle for getting power in one's own State, and only by assuming the point of view of looking at the interests of an aggregation of states or of all states, is it possible to deal with the problems of peace, not in terms of international equilibria, but of popular control on international politics and on a democratic supra-national governance.

Every assembly of peoples, like every assembly of individuals, requires common institutions, requires an organization. Outside of that, all is decided by force. To wish that Europe stays in peace is to wish that a social body subsists on conventions and agreements: in both cases there must be a coercive force that unites the wills, plans the movements, makes the interests common and the commitments firm (Saint-Simon C.-H. de, Thierry A., 173, vol. 1).

According to Saint-Simon, for Europe to be pacified it is necessary "to bring Europe's peoples into a single political body, each of them retaining its national independence" (Saint-Simon C.-H. de, Thierry A., 153, vol. 1). European institutions should be modelled on those of the British monarchy and hinge on a European Parliament "placed above all national governments and endowed with the power to pass judgement on their international disputes" (Saint-Simon C.-H. de, Thierry A., 197, vol. 1). They have therefore a supranational character, but not all of the requisites of a federal state.

Is it a utopia? A similar idea had been in place in the feudal era, when Europe was a society united in common institutions. The limit of the feudal constitution consisted, in Saint-Simon's opinion, in its hierarchical and authoritarian character. Gradually, the feudal institutions were replaced by new institutions based on the principles of free government. Saint-Simon proposes to found on these same principles also the process of Europe's reorganization. He believes that the first nucleus of the European union will be formed by Great Britain and France, and it will later expand to the rest of Europe, as the conditions for establishing a parliamentary regime will mature in the other countries too.

Although Saint-Simon's project is vague in some aspects (a vagueness due to the fact that it is not a politically-operational project), it represents an amazing proof of how the problems of international organization could be dealt with in the era of democracy and nationalism. Peace was to be pursued through a democratic and supranational power centre, ruling on a group of independent nations.

Chapter Four

Federalism and the Criticism of the Limits of the National State in the 1800s

4.1. PROUDHON'S AND FRANTZ'S FEDERALISM AND THE NEGATION OF THE NATIONAL STATE

The political current prevailing in the 18th century has favoured the establishment of the national principle. The federalist point of view, which, as we have seen, was also present at the same time, albeit with no possibility to assert itself, was able to show the negative aspects of this phase of European history and the limits of the national State. Pierre-Joseph Proudhon (1809–1865) thought ill of the formation of the Italian state, and Constantin Frantz (1817–1891) felt the same of the formation of the German one; both of them, contrary to the prevailing opinion of their time, were considering the national principle and the unitary state not as factors enhancing democracy, but as new forms of oppression, not as factors of peace, but as sources of disputes of unprecedented violence between States.

On the Italian unification Proudhon wrote:

A state of 26 million souls, as Italy would be, is a State where all provincial and municipal liberties are forfeited to the advantage of a higher power, which is the government. There, every locality must keep silent, l'*esprit de clocher* is brought to silence: with the exception of the day of the elections, in which the citizen makes its sovereignty visible by writing a name on the ballot, the community is absorbed into the central power [. . .] The fusion, in one word, i.e. the annihilation of individual nationalities where citizens live and feel different, into one abstract nationality, where people cannot breathe and do not know one another any more: that's unity! — And concludes: — And who benefits from this regime of unity? The people? No, the upper classes (Proudhon P.-J., 1979, 8–9).

Proudhon is critical of the national principle, that is to say, the fusion of state and nation. With surprising clear-sightedness, in a page published after his death in the collection of fragments *France et Rhin*, in which the result of his long and intellectually laborious reflection on the national question seems to be concentrated, a truth emerges in full light that only today, in the presence of the historical decline of the national state and of the regional thrusts that are evident everywhere in Europe, is possible to fully appreciate.

> Today's French nation is composed of at least twenty different nations, whose character, as observed in people and peasants, is still quite strongly defined [. . .] The Frenchman is a conventional entity, he does not exist. [. . .] So wide a nation cannot hold together but by the use of force. A permanent army serves this purpose above all. Take its support away from the administration and central police and France will fall into federalism. Local attractions prevail (Proudhon P.-J., 1959, 594–595).

What Proudhon is implying is that there exists a *spontaneous* nationality, which is the result of the natural ties between local communities and their territory and culture, and an *organized* nationality, which is the artificial result of the ties between the state and the individuals living on its territory, and is the expression of the need for social and cultural uniformity and for exclusive loyalty the bureaucratic and centralized state has. In this way, he gave an important contribution to the understanding of the nationality-principle, explaining it as a myth whose purpose is to justify the unitary democratic state born out of the French Revolution, which supports itself on a permanent army requiring mandatory conscription, on a centralized bureaucratic and police apparatus, and on the fusion of state and nation.

Likewise, Frantz showed how nations are not "natural types" but "historical formations, a feature they share with the state," and how they change in history, as state boundaries do (Frantz C., 1879, 346). In such a way, he proved wrong the pretence by the unified Germany's political class to present the unitary experience of the German people as a fact already in existence in a very remote past.

Both Proudhon and Frantz were able to foresee that the explosive mixture represented by the fusion of state and nation would increase the states' aggressiveness and war-tendency, transforming them in "war machines." In particular, they sensed the disruptive potential of establishing the national principle in Central and Eastern Europe, where it was impossible to accurately draw state boundaries according to that principle. They understood that Europe's organization in national states would eventually break the balance of powers, would cause an increase of international tensions and would mar the continent in a series of "national wars."

As the establishment of the national principle was driving the states to transform themselves into centralized, closed, hostile and war-leaning groups, the spreading of the industrial revolution was tending to increase and intensify social relations and to unify them over ever-wider areas; there was the necessity to form new economic spaces, politically organized and of continental dimensions. His perception of this historical tendency let Frantz foresee the decline of the system of European states, faced with the rise of the United States and Russia to the rank of world powers. A federal unification was the only alternative for Europe to become a "third power" and compete at equal conditions with the powers of continental dimensions.

As an alternative to Germany's unification, Frantz was calling for a new European federal order, constructed around a German core. In fact, Germany is, according to Schelling's (1775–1854) expression, "a people of peoples" and is therefore better fitted to structure itself according to the multinational and federal principle of peaceful coexistence of several peoples, rather than to transform itself into a bureaucratic and centralized state. A German federation could then constitute the first core of a new international order, bound to extend itself to the rest of Europe and to transform the force relations among the states into relations founded on right. Like Proudhon, Frantz insists on the complementarity of the community-oriented and the cosmopolitan aspects that federalism has.

> While federalism, on the one hand, takes us to operate on a wider space, — he writes — on the other it develops local life, the communes, the corporations, the associations [. . .] We may state with certainty that the future will promote on the one hand the cosmopolitan ideas, and on the other the community-oriented and cooperative ideas (Frantz C., 1878, 206).

However, altogether Frantz's federalism is marked by his longing for some aspects of a pre-national society, and his rejection of the national principle can be seen more as a way to give continuity to the universal order pursued by the medieval Empire, than as the overcoming (in the dialectical meaning of this expression) of the national state.

Instead, Proudhon's political federalism aims at an integral realization of the principle of popular sovereignty proclaimed by the French Revolution and written down in constitutional texts, but made empty by centralization, which places the citizen at the service of the state. In a page of *Contradictions politiques,* Proudhon's communitarian ideal, which constitutes an essential component of his federalism, is expressed with great vigour. It is embodied in people's aspiration to actively participate in the many aspects of the life of the Commune, the state's basic cell, and to assert its autonomy:

> The Commune is by its very essence [. . .] a sovereign body. As such, the Commune has the right to self-govern, to administer itself, to raise taxes, to dispose of its properties and its revenues, to create schools for its youngsters, to appoint teachers, to institute its own police corps, to have its *gendarmerie*, to appoint judges, to have its newspapers, its meetings, its special associations, its warehouses, its price-lists, its bank, etc. The Commune takes deliberations, issues ordinances: what prevents it from making laws for itself? It has its church, its religious ceremonies, its freely elected clergy; it publicly discusses, in the municipal council, in its newspapers or in its clubs, everything pertaining to its interests or inflaming its ideas [. . .] There is no middle road: the Commune will be sovereign or it will be a mere branch-office, either all or nothing (Proudhon P.-J., 1952, 245–246).

The central government versus local government relation typical of the national state is reversed. The Commune is considered the main center for the organization of collective life: it is awarded powers, like making laws and raising taxes, keeping public order and appointing judges, traditionally awarded to the national government. If federalism is a political formula that demands to attribute to the smaller-communities' bodies a greater number of powers than ever before, it also allows to organize political power at all the levels where social life takes place, from the lowest (the territorial and functional community) to the highest (the human kind), so that society be subject at the same time to a "law of unity" and a "law of divergence," and obey at the same time a "centripetal movement" and a "centrifugal movement." "The result of this dualism is to make it possible one day that, through the federation of free forces and the decentralization of authority, all the states, big and small, compound the advantages of unity and liberty, of economy and power, of a cosmopolitan spirit and a patriotic sentiment" (Proudhon P.-J., 1861, 127). Federalism thus is a political formula of universal significance, "the political form of humanity" (Proudhon P.-J., 1982, 288, vol. 2).

However, he considers "contradictory" the idea of a "universal confederation."

> Even Europe would be too large to form a single confederation; it could form only a confederation of confederations [. . .] Thus each nationality would recover its liberty; and a European balance of power would be achieved—an idea foreseen by all political theorists and statesmen, but impossible to realize among great powers with unitary constitutions (Proudhon P.-J., 1979, 53).

Proudhon uses indifferently the terms federation and confederation, which in a more rigorous scientific language have opposite meanings. But confusion is not only verbal. He was not aware of the new form of state born with the Philadelphia Convention. He was not in a position to figure out the functioning of a federation that allows political power to be organized on several autonomous levels, coordinated among them and limiting each other. He believed that "the contract of federation had the purpose, in general terms, of guaranteeing to the federated states their sovereignty" (Proudhon P.-J., 1979, 41); hence, to ensure the subordination of the central authority to the member states. Therefore, the contract of federation, "instead of absorbing the federated states and provincial and municipal authorities within a central authority," aims at reducing "the role of the centre to that of general initiation, of providing guarantees and supervising, and make the execution of its orders subject to the approval of the federated governments and their responsible agents"(Proudhon P.-J., 1979, 49). From an institutional point of view, his political theory has a confederal character. However, he conceived federalism as the most efficient instrument for asserting law over force in the relations among social groups, for bringing about peace among nations, and, in sum, for organizing humankind in a cosmopolitan order and at the same time compounding unity with diversity both in the relations among states and among social groups. According to Proudhon, democracy on the national plane, as instituted by the French Revolution, is not, in principle, in contradiction with democracy on the local and supranational levels; hence, is not in contradiction with the creation of democratic institutions provided with independent powers at all the levels where social life is carried out. Believing that democracy can only express itself on one government level is the most serious limit of the national thinking.

In 1862, drawing a balance of his political itinerary, Proudhon wrote:

> Whereas in 1840 I started out with anarchy, the result of my criticism of the idea of government, I ended up with the federation, the necessary basis for a law of the European peoples, and, later on, for an organization of all of the states" (Proudhon P.-J., 1874–1875, 220. vol. 12).

His federal point of view allowed Proudhon to denounce the pathological, hence transitional, character of the political formula of the national state. The decline of the historical role of that type of state is made apparent today in Europe by the regional unification process and the trend to decentralization, and in the world by its subordination to the actors of the globalization process. The model of a closed and centralized state, which organizes the division instead of the unity of humankind, and pursues monism instead of social pluralism, is no longer adequate to the development of the productive forces and to the new dimensions taken by the problems of both domestic and international politics. All this proves the prophetic value of Proudhon's statement that "the twentieth century will open the age of federations, or else humanity will undergo another purgatory of a thousand years" (Proudhon P.-J., 1979, 68–69).

4.2. PROUDHON AND THE CRITICISM OF THE LIMITS OF LIBERALISM, DEMOCRACY AND SOCIALISM

Thus, federalism qualifies itself as the political theory that allows to solve the problems left open by the French Revolution with its assertion of the principle of "one and indivisible Republic," and to overcome the contradictions of the unitary national state model. The French Revolution has emancipated the nation by recognizing popular sovereignty, but the principles of centralization of political power and nationalism have proved to be in contrast with liberty, democracy and socialism. That is the reason why, Proudhon writes, "Who says liberty says federation, or says nothing. Who says republic says federation, or again says nothing. Who says socialism says federation, or again says nothing" (Proudhon P.-J., 1979, 80).

In the first place, Proudhon shows how the structure of the unitary state reduces to an empty juridical formula the principle of separation of powers, the fundamental guarantee of free government. There is an unmendable contradiction between the principle of separation of powers and that of centralization. While the first is based on the autonomy of certain power centres (the Parliament, local bodies, etc.) from the central government, and therefore on the presence of counterbalances, opposition, antagonism between state powers, the second does not tolerate any centre of political initiative outside of the central government.

The idea of a limitation to the state, where the principle of centralization of groups reigns supreme, is thus an inconsistency, not to say an absurdity. There is no other limitation to the state but the one it imposes on itself, leaving to the municipal or individual initiative a few things it does not care for the time being. But, as its range of action is unlimited, it may happen that it wants to extend it to things that it had despised until then; and as it is the strongest, as it never speaks and acts but in the name of the public interest, not only will it get what it asks for, but before the public opinion and the courts it will even be judged right (Proudhon P.-J., 1952, 246).

In a unitary state, political struggle is waged in one institutional context for seizing one power, not subject to any effective limitation and arbitrator of the Constitution itself.

Secondly, Proudhon is critical of the Jacobin-type democracy, which has brought to perfection the State's centralization.

> Democracy has little regard of individual liberties and the observance of the law, because it is unable to govern in conditions different from those of unity, which is nothing else but despotism. [. . .] Democracy is above all centralizing and unitary; it abhors federalism" (Proudhon P.-J., 1979, 81).

This type of democracy that gives sovereignty to the people, seen as an entity closed in itself, uniform, indivisible, and that condemns as an attack to popular sovereignty everything that may divide, differentiate, place one in front of the other the wills concurring to shape up the will of the nation, should not, properly speaking, call itself democracy, because all the social groups, all the cities and the other local bodies, being subject to the same authority and the same administration, lose their autonomy.

In the social contract, as imagined by Rousseau and the Jacobins, the citizen divests himself of sovereignty, and the town and the department and province above it, absorbed by central authority, are no longer anything but agencies under direct ministerial control.

> The consequences soon make themselves felt: the citizen and the town are deprived of all dignity, the state's depredations multiply, and the burden on the taxpayer increases in proportion. It is no longer the government that is made for the people; it is the people who are made for the government. Power invades everything, dominates everything, for ever, for always, without end (Proudhon P.-J., 1979, 59).

A democracy that works at the national level only, without a base of local self-government, is a nominal democracy, because it controls from the top and strangles the communities, that is to say, the concrete life of men. The principle itself of popular sovereignty turns into a myth, whose purpose is to legitimise the people's subordination to the central power.

Thirdly, Proudhon is not, like the socialists of his time, critical of the capitalist exploitation only, but also of the authoritarian and centralizing aspects of socialism. He denounces the mystification concealed behind the expression "collective property" and intends to demonstrate that even if property is transferred from private citizens to the community represented by the state, its fundamental fault, that is the awarding of property to some, who appropriate the fruit of the work of the others, is not eliminated. Changing the holder of property would not substantially change the nature of that institution; indeed, it would end up "reproducing, on an inverted plane, all its contradictions." That is to say, there would be a transformation of production relations, but the control and management of production means would be given to a particular social group, hence exploitation would not be eliminated. Arguing against the utopian socialism, the "crude communism" according to Marx' expression, Proudhon observes:

> How strange! The systematic *community*, reflection of the negation of property, is conceived under the direct influence of the prejudice of property; and property is what is found at the bottom of all communistic theories. The members of a *community*, it is true, have nothing of their own; but the *community* is a proprietor, and proprietor not only of goods, but also of people and their wills (Proudhon P.-J., 1926, 326).

On the other hand, the merging of economic power with political power constitutes the premise for a new and more oppressive form of dictatorship:

> Of all prejudices, the one the communists cherish most is dictatorship. Dictatorship of industry, dictatorship of commerce, dictatorship of thought, dictatorship in social life and in private life, dictatorship everywhere; that is the dogma [. . .] After all individual wills are suppressed, they concentrate them in a supreme individuality, which is the expression of collective thinking and, like Aristotle's motionless motor, gives the start to all subordinate activities (Proudhon P.-J., 1923, 301, vol. 2).

4.3. PROUDHON AND INTEGRAL FEDERALISM

The negative part of Proudhon's thought is then constituted by a double negation: negation of the state's authoritarianism and centralism, and negation of the exploitation by man over man. One of the most interesting aspects of his thought is represented by his "integral" conception of federalism. In fact, beside his political federalism, he formulated the idea of an economic and social federalism, necessary for limiting the powers of the state and of the privileged groups that support its power.

> All my economic ideas, developed over the last twenty-five years, can be defined in these three words: *agro-industrial federation*; all my political views may be reduced to a parallel formula: *political federation* or *decentralization;*

[. . .] all my hopes for the present and the future are contained in a third term, a corollary of the first two: *progressive federation* (Proudhon P.-J., 1979, 74).

For Proudhon, economic federalism does not coincide with the abolition of property. His idea of property, considered at the same time as "theft" and as a condition for "liberty," seemed contradictory to somebody. For presenting it, I will follow Mario Albertini's (1974) analysis. We have seen that Proudhon, in his criticism of the limits of centralizing collectivism and of the state's property of the means of production, has highlighted how the individualistic feature of property, consisting in awarding to some the means of production, cannot be eliminated. From such a viewpoint, we can understand why Proudhon assigns to property the task:

> to act as a counterbalance to public power, to balance the state, and in this way to assure individual liberty. [In fact], in order for the citizen to be something in the state, it is not enough that he be free as a person; it is necessary that his personality rest, like that of the state, on a solid piece of matter that he possesses in full sovereignty, as the State has the sovereignty in the public sphere (Proudhon P.-J., 1866, 138).

The property right appears therefore as the condition for individual autonomy and for assigning to each the fruit of his work. Property must be studied in the framework of the dialectical relations between state and society. Its role is to assure the autonomy of the economic and social life from the state.

> [Whilst]"the power of the state is a concentrating power (give it the start and every individuality will soon disappear, absorbed by the collectivity; and society falls into communism), [property instead] is a decentralizing power, because it is absolute, anti-dispotical, anti-unitary. In it there is the principle of every federation: that is why property, autocratic in its essence, transposed in a political society immediately becomes republican" (Proudhon P.-J., 1866, 144).

Proudhon acknowledges the existence of individual egoism, in which he actually finds a positive aspect, and in any case he is not under the illusion that it can be eliminated. The fact remains, however, that an important thing that cannot be eliminated is awarding to some the means of production. Thus, he confronts the problem of how to eliminate privilege or, in particular, the negative aspects of social relations based on property. The property of the means of production may be in the hands of those who make use of them, and that does not produce any form of injustice or exploitation. But property may be separated from work, giving rise to the *droit d'aubaine*, i.e. to that distortion of property consisting in appropriating the fruit of the work of other people. This is the aspect of property which must be abolished if force relations are to be eliminated from society. The abolition of the *droit d'aubaine* or, to use a more common expression, of surplus-value, is realized by awarding the possession of the means of production to individuals or groups that make use of them. Once the surplus-value is eliminated and property is put under a social control, every form of authoritarianism is bound to disappear and the power of the state to be constrained by efficient limitations.

In line with his anti-authoritarian and decentralized idea of economic management, Proudhon works out an organizational model of factories and enterprises that can be defined as workers' self-management. The most important principles this self-management is based on are the following: all workers are co-owners; all positions are elective and regulations are subject to the members' approval; everybody has the right to fill every position; salaries are in proportion to the nature of the position.

As far as agriculture is concerned, Proudhon is for individual property and the establishment of rural communes, with the task to distribute the land to those who cultivate it and to reorganize it according to scopes of co-operation and social utility. The workers associated in the basic productive units (self-managed enterprises, rural communes) constitute the basic cells of the agricultural-industrial federation; in it, the property of the means of production is awarded at the same time to the organization of the economic society as a whole, to each region, to every association of workers and to every worker. The agricultural-industrial federation, thus, allows it to reorganize the productive structures under the control of the workers, associated in many basic, autonomous groups, while solidarity among them is assured by their federal tie. This type of organization of society and economy makes it possible to realize what may be called today a democratic decentralized plan, founded on the needs of the territorial and functional communities. In fact, when a plan is decided at the center with no real relation with the requirements of local communities, it is not only authoritarian, but also inefficient, because it is not based on the real needs of the people.

Now, the federal economic and social organization offers a formula that permits to avert the double danger represented by the arbitrary dominance of capitalist groups and by that, as much arbitrary, of ruling groups justifying their power in the name of communism. This type of plan and self-management appear to give the working class an association form capable of taking away from the dominant groups the levers of political, economic and ideological direction, and of liberating the social energies necessary for subordinating capital to labour. Here we may note that Proudhon, trying to figure out a future society freed from dominance and exploitation, presents it, according to the situation of his time, as a society of workers and peasants, who will have subjected to their control the means of production and will have eliminated the ruling classes that had their privileges based on capital and unearned income. The limit of this point of view lies in the fact, already perceived by Marx (*Outlines of the Critique of Political Economy, Notebook V*), that the people liberation process and the creation of community-oriented social relations cannot come about without an in-depth transformation of the society structure, that eliminates the roles themselves of worker and peasant, as made possible today by the "scientific and technological revolution" (Richta R., 1969). It allows one to progressively eliminate manual work and the scarcity of material goods, and with it the competition for the necessary; therefore, it lets us think of the progressive elimination of alienated work as a concrete possibility.

4.4 FEDERALISM IN THE ITALIAN RISORGIMENTO

The figure of Giuseppe Mazzini, which offers one of the highest examples of the problems, the aspirations, the illusions, the ambiguities and the contradictions of any national movement, rightly occupies a pre-eminent place in the history of the federalist idea, for the strong supra-national component of his political thought. Albeit he devoted all his energies to Italy's unification, he always remained loyal to the idea of the unity of Europe and the whole human kind. In order to explain this seeming contradiction, one has to keep in mind the strong idealization of the concept of nation that is peculiar to the first stages of every national movement. That was an essential incentive for a kind of political activity that had no sound foothold in reality and helped fill the gap separating thought from the possibility to put it in practice. For Mazzini, the terms nation and humanity are not contradictory, but complementary. He believed that, when nationality had triumphed, all cause of war would disappear.

Every nation—one can read in his last writing—has a mission, a special task in the collective work, a special attitude to accomplish that task. That is its mark, its baptism, its legitimacy. Every nation is a worker for humanity, it works for it, so that the common end be attained for the advantage of all; if it betrays its task and it gets corrupted into egoism, it declines and inevitably undergoes a more or less long expiation, proportionate to the degree of its guilt (Mazzini G., 260–261, vol. 93).

Mazzini considered national egoism as the betrayal of a principle that was to lead to the unity of mankind. Indeed, he believed that the national principle would coincide with the end of the Christian era, based on individualism, and the start of a new era in which the unity and solidarity of the whole mankind would be realized. Europe was for Mazzini the place where the conditions existed for opening this new historical era.

> The European political order had by necessity to come before any other work. And that order could not be brought about but by the peoples: by peoples that, freely made brothers in one faith, all believing in a common end, had each a precise task, a special mission in the endeavour. For Europe to be able to really proceed, to come to a new synthesis and to consecrate to carry it out all the forces that are wearing themselves off today in an internal fight, its charter has to be rewritten. The question of nationality was [. . .] the European sharing of the work. Anyway, the question of nationality was for me the question that would have given its name to the century. Italy, as I regarded and cherished it, could be, and will be, the initiator if, freeing itself from the vile and immoral gang which dominates it today, will one day acknowledge its duty and its power (Mario J.W., 214–215).

His political vision differentiates itself from cosmopolitanism, which he joined before founding the *Giovane Italia (Young Italy)* movement (1831), in that he believed that national organization was the vehicle for realizing universal liberty and brotherhood. The *Giovane Europa (Young Europe)* represents the first (1834) of several experiments made in the 18th century to build an International of the peoples. It was an alliance of the republicans of three countries: Italy, Germany and Poland. Mazzini devised it as an international organization aimed at uniting the nationalist movements, to struggle for the nations' emancipation against the old Europe of the Holy Alliance of monarchs, of conservatism, of privilege, of division and discord. Europe's reconstruction on national bases should have marked the beginning of a new era in the course of which human solidarity and brotherhood among peoples had to develop, virtues that would have allowed all European peoples to cooperate for the progress of the whole human kind. In article 19 of the "Giovane Europa"'s statute, drafted by Mazzini himself, one reads: "Humanity will not be really constituted but when all peoples composing it, having acquired the free exercise of their sovereignty, will be associated in a republican federation" (Mazzini G., 11, vol. 3). There is to say that Mazzini was assigning to Italy, the nation he loved most, the mission to accomplish European unity. But Italy's role as the leading people did not look to him in contrast with the idea of a free association among peoples. Italy's primacy does not have an imperialistic character, only a spiritual one. The *Giovane Europa*'s project remained the expression of an aspiration that never translated into an active organization on the international plane. Bolton King, one of Mazzini's best biographers, wrote: "When one remembers that its vast scheme of transformation was the work of a few young exiles, it reads like a pure rhodomontade. Mazzini himself recognised afterwards that the plan was too embracing to lead to practical results" (King B., 63).

For coming to an overall evaluation of the European and supra-national aspects of Mazzini's thought, the realistic elements of his political vision have to be separated from the utopian. A realistic character has his anticipation of the central place that the national problem would have in the 1800s, and a formidable intuition is his idea that it was possible to create new unitary states based on the fusion of state and nation. But it is completely out of reality his idea of the nation based on duty and mission, and of European unity based on a religious sentiment of solidarity among nations. The reality that little by little unfolded was that the national states, like monarchies, could not succeed in finding a natural harmony among them, and behind the "sovereign nation" the *raison d'état* continued to operate with its traditional requirements of security and power. One can rightly say that on balance Europe's organization in national states has been a failure: it deepened the divisions among states and was a decisive factor in contributing to cause the world wars. Mazzini's limit, and the limit of every national thought, consists in having failed to foresee those consequences. The contradiction between nation and humanity, between nation and Europe, that Mazzini was under the illusion to have overcome, cannot be settled in reality as long as national sovereignty is maintained.

The goal of European unity always remained in Mazzini's mind a vague idea, which never materialized in a precise definition in institutional terms. He always considered the unitary national state as the highest form of organization of society. Therefore, he was against any form of power decentralization, and at the same time considered the independence of European nations as the necessary condition for carrying out the mission they were called upon by the divine providence: to give their contribution to the progress of mankind. Actually, the idea of overcoming national sovereignty was unthinkable in the theoretical horizon of national thought. Lacking a sound knowledge of federal institutions, every time he dealt with the problem of Europe's future political arrangement he could not but envisage it in the traditional terms of European balance. Despite this, the lasting merit of Mazzini's European lesson lies in the idea that democracy cannot rest confined in the national space without degenerating, and in the aspiration to humanity and a Europe where violence among nations is rooted out, so that peace and solidarity among peoples could thrive. While Mazzini's merit is to have pointed out these goals, he was wrong in proposing the way to get there. On this point the federalist theory has given a fundamental contribution: the road leading to peace is not the cooperation among sovereign nations, but the subordination of national sovereignties to a higher power.

In the Europe of the 1800s the term federalism was rarely used with reference to the organization of political power created with the Constitution of the United States. It is normally associated with the general idea of a pluralistic unity of a system of states. For example, for Giuseppe Ferrari (1811–1876) the federal principle represents the guiding thread of the entire European history: "Europe is constantly federal." In the course of history, "all of the states in Europe have been marching on the same road without knowing it (Ferrari G., 597–598). The federal principle is opposed to the unitary, which is prevailing in the East. Federalism constitutes the central concept in his philosophy of history and represents the distinctive feature of European civilization, which finds its expression in pluralism, in the principle of liberty and in the opposition to any attempt at political unification. Interpreted in such vague terms, the word federalism cannot connote any historically-determined political or social situation. It simply indicates a constant feature of European history. Consequently, there is not even the need to pose the problem of compounding unity with diversity in Europe through appropriate institutions: such composition is realized already.

Carlo Cattaneo (1801–1869) is the only thinker and politician in the Risorgimento that may be considered as a forerunner of European federalism as conceived in the 20th century, in the sense that his federalism has a precise and well-defined structure under the institutional aspect. But the modernity of his federalist thinking lies not only in his knowledge of the structure and functioning of federal institutions, but also in having seen the illiberal and authoritarian limits of the institutions of the unitary national state, that is to say, in having conceived the federal model as the negation of the oppressive and centralizing aspects of the unitary state.

Cattaneo conceived federalism as a technique that allows for a liberal-democratic regime to be organized on wider spaces than the national state, and to decentralize political power. He defined federalism as "the theory of liberty, the only possible theory of liberty" (Cattaneo C., 1949–1956, 122, vol. 2). In fact, federal institutions allow one to put in place the most efficient form of limitation of political power through the subordination of a plurality of independent states to a higher, but limited, power centre. Through the federal principle, which from a technical point of view consists in "coordinating the two legislative orders of the Union as a whole and of the individual states," it is possible to get a juridical regulation of social activities, from the lowest scale (the region) to the highest (the human kind), by awarding to each decision-making centre the competences corresponding to the needs and the problems of the various communities.

> Every people—Cattaneo wrote—may have many interests it has to take care of together with other peoples; but there are interests that it alone can take care of, because it alone feels them, because it alone understands them. And in addition there is also in every people the awareness of its being, also the pride of its name, also the jealousy of its ancestors' land. Hence the federal right, i.e. the

right of the peoples; which must have its place beside the right of the nation, beside the right of humanity (Cattaneo C.,1892–1901, 404, vol. 3).

These "peoples," distinct from "nations," are the regional peoples. The federal state stands out as the only political formula allowing a pluralistic unity to be realized, thus compounding unity with liberty. "Only in the way Switzerland and the United States did—he wrote—can unity and liberty be compounded" (Cattaneo C.,1892–1901, 142, vol. 1). Liberty is then the result of a double limitation of political power: a limitation within the states through decentralization, and a limitation in international relations through the states' subordination to a supra-national government.

Federalism gives Cattaneo an autonomous judging criterion for all the important questions of his time, and the federal solution is applied to the main problems, from that of Italian unification (until 1848 Cattaneo believed that it was possible to transform Austria in a federal sense, so that room could be given to the autonomy of Lombardy-Venetia; later he became a supporter of Italian federalism) to that of the peace in Europe. We have seen the reasons why federalism never became a principle of political action nor could it have any influence on the historical events in the Europe of the 1800s, except in marginal situations like Switzerland. But the real limit of federalism, seen as a theory of liberty, lies in its abstract and historically-undetermined advocating of particular values and institutions, with no consideration given to the internal and international conditions of the political struggle, which in certain situations (Switzerland and the United States) allow for and in others (the national states in the European continent) impede its establishment. However, negating the unitary state's pretence to present itself as the highest form of political organization of humanity lets Cattaneo place himself in a perspective especially favourable for perceiving the limits of the national State and foreseeing the causes of the impending crisis of the national state.

Cattaneo's greatest merit is having vigorously denounced the authoritarian nature of the unitary state, which strangles the autonomy of local and regional communities, sacrificing, in the name of an artificial uniformity imposed from above, the variety and richness of local cultures and institutions. One of the favourite targets of his polemic is the constitutional arrangement of the French state:

In the shadow of the gallows and the *gendarmerie*, France's prefectoral government is able to manoeuvre by telegraphic orders 86 puppet theatres of 400 thousand puppets each. Until the departments will become cantons with their own administration, liberty in France will always be an absurdity; because who waits for orders from Paris is not free in Versailles (Cattaneo C.,1892–1901, 275, vol. 1).

There is no substantial difference between a monarchical and a republican centralism. Both are equally oppressive and levelling.

> It does not matter that the telegraph imposes to the submissive and silent departments the order of an emperor, a king or a president; the destiny of the multitude of Frenchmen, outside of the Paris walls, was always obedience (Cattaneo C., 1973, 243–244).

On the other hand, he does not believe that the spreading of the national principle will automatically eliminate the old causes of conflict among states. "Outside of the federal right, we will always be jealous, discord and unhappy" (Cattaneo C., 1892–1901, 408 vol. 1). In other terms, if the European nations will ever have to live in peace, it will be necessary to replace the international right with the federal right, and the European system of powerful states, based on the states' absolute sovereignty, with a supra-national government. So, the prophetic statement which closes his book on the Milan insurrection of 1848 ("We will have a true peace when we will have the United States of Europe" (1973, 244)) takes on the meaning of a warning to the prevailing political currents of his time, all of them anxious to create new national states, and is an indication of a new route for building a real peace.

4.5. THE MOVEMENT FOR PEACE AND FOR EUROPEAN UNITY IN THE 19TH CENTURY

In the course of the 1800s, in the United States first, then in Great Britain and later on in the European continent a peace movement was established, articulated in small associations, initially of local dimension, then national and international. Some of the associations were short-lived, others were more stable. But the spreading of the peace movement proves that it was interpreting deep-seated historical demands. Its main component was of a Christian inspiration. In particular, the Quaker sect promoted the movement in the Anglo-Saxon countries. But also currents of a political character, drawing their inspiration from the liberal and socialist ideologies, joined it. The "Peace Societies" carried on a propaganda activity against the horrors of war and for international solidarity, through the publication of journals and the organization of international conferences, which gathered pacifists coming from many countries.

After the Peace Congress of 1848, held in Brussels, a permanent organization was established: the Committee of the Peace Congress. Still famous is the congress that was held in Paris in 1849, presided over by Victor Hugo (1802–1885), who in his opening address called for an era of peace, in which

> war will look as absurd and impossible between Paris and London and between Petersburg and Berlin, between Vienna and Turin, as it would be impossible and would seem absurd today between Rouen and Amiens, between Boston and Philadelphia. A day will come when you France, you Russia, you Italy, you England, you Germany, you all, nations of the continent, without losing your distinctive qualities and your glorious individuality, will coalesce into a greater entity, and will constitute the European fraternity, [in which] cannon balls and bombs will be replaced by votes, by the universal suffrage of peoples, by the venerable arbitration of a supreme, sovereign senate [. . .]. A day will come when we shall see those two immense groups, the United States of America and the United States of Europe, stretching out their hands across the sea (Hugo V., 1875, 388).

There is also to mention the congress convened in Geneva in 1867, in which great figures participated, like Michail Bakunin (1814–1876), Louis Blanc (1811–1882), Giuseppe Garibaldi (1807–1882), Victor Hugo, John Stuart Mill (1806–1873), Edgar Quinet (1803–1875). One of the animator of the congress was Charles Lemonnier (1806–1891), who proposed the institution of the League for Peace and Liberty, whose objective was to create, on the constitutional model of the United States and Switzerland, the United States of Europe, a formula he adopted as the title of a periodical he was the director of. A little earlier, in Lausanne, the International Working Men's Association (later called the First International) had met, which approved a resolution in favour of the United States of Europe.

Around the end of the century, the initiatives in support of peace heightened. From 1889 on, after the crisis caused by the Franco-Prussian war, the Peace Congresses started again to be held every year, and in their works they (in particular the one held in Rome in 1891) called again for the objective of the United States of Europe. In 1891 the peace movement constituted in Bern its international centre, named Peace Bureau. Jurists and economists devoted meetings and scientific papers to the problems of the international order. At the same time, the first forms of international organizations were established: the Universal Postal Union (1874) and the International Telegraph Union (1875). In 1889 the Inter-Parliamentary Union was instituted in Paris, which fought especially for the approval of the principle of arbitration. Following the Peace Conference held in The Hague in 1899, the first international Court was established, which should have had to settle by arbitration the international disputes.

There is also to mention that within the peace movement, in the United States, a current emerged which was calling for a world federation. In 1910 the New York Peace Society gave birth to the World Federation Committee, which in 1912 took the name of World Federation League. Within the peace movement, then, a specifically federalist current emerges, which intends to apply the US constitutional model to the international plane for realizing peace in Europe and the world. What this current had in common with the rest of the peace movement is a utopian political conception that identified the obstacle to peace in ideas and not in the actual structure of international relations, which had to be changed through an appropriate political strategy.

These ideas were reflecting the fact that a growing number of problems could only be faced and solved on the international plane. However, the movements for peace and European unity did not have the means for countering the establishment in governments and political parties of nationalism and militarism, which grew in Europe because of the crisis of the European balance of power. The influence of European and international ideals faded more and more, in parallel with the establishment of nationalism and the inclusion in the boundaries of the national state of all political currents, including those of internationalist inspiration. Consequently, the pacifist organizations were run over by the growing international anarchy that was dragging Europe towards the tragic epilogue of two world wars. The same fate suffered the Second International. The pacifists were incriminated as defeatists and their organizations were dissolved or anyway made unable to operate. In the crucial moment of war there is no room for any form of international solidarity.

4.6 SEELEY, THE CRISIS OF THE NATIONAL STATE AND THE FEDERALIST ALTERNATIVE

In the Anglo-Saxon peoples' culture and historical experience, there is an idea and an organizational form of the state that has allowed, as Lord Acton (1834–1902) wrote, "the coexistence of several nations under the same state," which "is a test as well as the best security of its freedom" (Dalberg-Acton J.E.E., 1909, 290). Instead, the consequence of the enforcement of the unitary principle, on which the state organization in the European continent is founded, is that the nation. In order to defend itself, "it overrules the rights and wishes of the inhabitants, absorbing their divergent interests into a fictitious unity; sacrifices their several inclinations and duties to the higher claim of nationality, and crushes all natural rights and all established liberties" (Dalberg-Acton J.E.E., 1909, 288). This viewpoint lets us perceive the limits of the exclusive nature of the national solidarity, ties, that do not tolerate the coexistence of any other loyalty to communities smaller and larger than the nation-state, a political entity that organizes the division instead of the unity of humankind, and pursues social monism instead of social pluralism.

The historical research of John R. Seeley (1834–1895) is based on a precise methodological choice that, in the wake of the thinking tradition of the theory of *raison d'état*, assigns to the state a central role in history. In his most important book, *The Expansion of England* (1883), he writes:

> If we analyse this vague sum-total which we call civilisation, we shall find that a large part of it is [. . .] the result of the union of men in civil communities or states [. . .]. I consider therefore that history has to do with the state [. . .] History is not concerned with individuals except in their capacity of members of a state (Seeley J.R., 1909, 6–8).

Seeley's predominant interest is addressed to the state's organizational forms that contain the secret of their capability to determine the course of history:

> Throughout the greater part of human history the process of state-building has been governed by strict conditions of space. For a long time no high organisation was possible except in very small states. In antiquity the good states were usually cities, and Rome herself when she became an Empire was obliged to adopt a lower organisation. In medieval Europe, states sprung up which were on a larger scale than those in antiquity, but for a long time these too were lower organisms and looked up to Athens and Rome with reverence as to the homes of political greatness. But through the invention of the representative system these states have risen to a higher level. We now see states with vivid political consciousness on territories of two hundred thousand square miles and in populations of thirty millions. A further advance is now being made. The federal system has been added to the representative system, and at the same time steam and electricity have been introduced. From these improvements has resulted the possibility of highly organised states on a yet larger scale. Thus Russia in Europe has already a population of near eighty millions on a territory of more than two millions of square miles, and the United States will have by the end of the century a population as large upon a territory of four millions of square miles. We cannot, it is true, yet speak of Russia as having a high type of organisation; she has her trials and her transformation to come; but the Union has shown herself able to combine free institutions in the fullest degree with boundless expansion [. . .] Russia and the United States will surpass in power the states now called great as much as the great country-states of the sixteenth century surpassed Florence (Seeley J.R., 1909, 347–350).

These are not new ideas. The emphasis given to the institutional innovations that allowed peoples to make progress on the road to ever-higher forms of political life, the distinction between assembly, representative and federal democracy, the stages in the enlargement of the democratic state's dimensions are theoretical acquisitions that date back to *The Federalist*. What is new, although not thoroughly analysed, is the idea that free government is an element contributing to "a good organization" of the state, therefore it gives it internal stability and influence on the international plane. But in particular what Seeley makes clear is the fact that behind the enlargement of the democratic state's dimensions there are powerful unifying forces, set in motion by the evolution of the mode of production, which, as made clear by the materialistic conception of history, determine "in the last instance" the state's structures. Behind the city-state there is the agricultural mode of production, behind the national state there is the expansion of trade and industrial production. Behind the federation of dimensions as great as an entire world region there is the second phase of the industrial revolution.

In the three decades preceding the outbreak of the first World War, industrial expansion received a strong thrust by the sizeable growth of available energy, thanks to the use of the electric motor and the petrol-fed engine, that gave an extraordinary impulse to mechanization of production, to the employment of new production techniques (e.g. the production line and the conveyer belt), to the introduction of mass production. Moreover, organic chemistry made it possible to use new synthetic products. But even more extraordinary was the revolution that affected the transport sector (motoring and aeronautics) and communications (radio and telephone), which had a crucial importance for what regards the progressive contraction of space and the growth of interdependence between peoples and states.

"The same inventions which make vast political unions possible"—Seeley observed—"tend to make states which are on the old scale of magnitude unsafe, insignificant, second-rate" (Seeley J.R., 1909, 88). Since 1883, Seeley not only forecast that the helm of world politics would pass into the hands of the two superpowers (Russia and the United States), but also that "such old European states, as France and Germany," would be "depressed into a second class" (Seeley J.R., 1909, 88), and that the same will happen to Great Britain. This is the phenomenon we usually call the decline of the national state.

The mighty shockwave emanating from the revolutionary changes in the mode of production hit the institutions of the national state. The developing production forces were pressing for the enlargement of production and exchange relations, while the material base of the European states was becoming inadequate for the possibilities of development the modern industrial society was expressing. The cause of the crisis of the national state lies therefore in the growing contradiction, which was already looming at around the end of the 19th century, between the tendency of the productive forces to organize themselves over wider spaces, and the national dimensions of political power. Whereas this tendency did not find obstacles in the immense spaces of the Tzars' Empire and of the United States, it was slowed down by Europe's political division and by the rivalry between national states, which were opposing the formation of a society, an economy and a political power on a European plane, that would have made it possible for Europeans to compete with the powers of regional dimensions and to continue to play a world role. However, this tendency, worsening the tensions among the states of the European system and driving them to look for "living space" beyond their borders, was condemning the national state to an inevitable historical decline.

The alternative that Seeley arrived at already in 1871 was the *United States of Europe*. This is the title of a lecture he delivered to the Peace Society in London. In tune with Kant's theory of war and peace and drawing from the lessons of Ranke's history-school, and more precisely from his theory of *raison d'état*, Seeley makes a reflection on the causes of war and on the routes leading to peace. In everybody's eyes there were the horrors of the Franco-Prussian war, the increasingly destructive potential of war and "the unrelieved fierceness of national antipathy" (Seeley J.R, 1989, 186). Seeley draws the conclusion that "scarcely any cause of war which operated in monarchical Europe will cease to operate in the popular Europe of the future; and that the wars of the peoples will be far more gigantic, more wasteful of blood and suffering, than ever were the wars of the kings" (Seeley J.R, 1989, 173). He spots the root of the crisis of the European power balance in the danger of Germany's hegemony over Europe:

> The history of the last two centuries shows that the combined force of all the European states is not always clearly superior to the force of one. Louis XIV and Napoleon were humbled with the greatest possible difficulty, and we begin to doubt at the present day whether Europe could effectively resist united Germany, if Germany should enter upon a path of ambition (Seeley J.R, 1989, 182).

If you add to that the mighty thrust the industrial revolution had given to the development of productive forces and to the overcoming of the state's national dimensions, you have together the essential elements explaining the reasons why Europe and the world had entered a new era.

So, Seeley poses himself, neither more nor less, the problem of "abolishing war." How to deal with this problem? "War will not be abolished until some other method of settling quarrels has been introduced" (Seeley J.R, 1989, 173). Such method is offered by the federal institutions. The United

States of America is the model. The political unity these institutions ensure is
the vehicle for establishing peace in Europe first, and then in the whole world:

> Europe constituted into a single state, with a federal executive and legislature,
> located in some central Washington! Famous states like England and France for-
> bidden to levy soldiers, and slowly shrinking into counties beside the federation,
> which steadily grows in majesty, and constantly absorbs by its gravitation the
> genius and ambition that were attached before to the different national govern-
> ments! Such a revolution in human affairs, I am perfectly well aware, has
> scarcely ever been witnessed.
>
> [For the European federation] is not merely an arrangement between govern-
> ments, but a real union of peoples, so I think it can never be attained by mere
> diplomatic methods, or by the mere action of governments, but only by a uni-
> versal popular movement, [which will have to become] large enough to impose
> the scheme upon governments that would in many cases be from instinctive in-
> terest bitterly hostile to it! (Seeley J.R, 1989, 182–185).

These are extraordinarily far-sighted intentions if one considers the times
when they were formulated; they forerun by seventy years the debates and the
theoretical studies which led to the birth of federalist movements. The difficulty implied in pursuing this objective, in an era in which peoples were in-
flamed by nationalist passions, made Seeley abandon the cause of the European federation, but not that of federalism. He became a supporter of the
transformation of the British Empire into a federation. *The Expansion of England* is not only a history work of the highest level. It is also the manifesto of
a political movement, the Imperial Federation League, which was constituted
in 1884, one year after the publication of Seeley's book. The thesis he maintains is that, had it been possible at the time of the American Revolution "to
give parliamentary representation to our colonists" in Westminster, "we might
easily have avoided" the war of independence. On this matter he quotes
Burke's (1729–1797) opinion, which "throws ridicule upon the notion of
summoning representatives from so vast a distance" (Seeley J.R., 1909, 87).
"Opposuit natura," he had regretfully noted, adding that it was impossible "to
remove the eternal barriers of the creation" (Burke E., 153, vol. 2).
    But now two new facts allow us to conclude that "this impediment exists
no longer" (Seeley J.R., 1909, 87). On the one hand,

> science has given to the political organism a new circulation, which is steam,
> and a new nervous system, which is electricity. These new conditions make it
> necessary to reconsider the whole colonial problem. [On the other], those very
> colonies, which then broke off from us, have since given the example of a fed-
> eral organisation, in which vast territories [. . .] are held easily in union with

older communities, and the whole enjoys in the fullest degree parliamentary freedom. The United States have solved a problem substantially similar to that which our old colonial system could not solve (Seeley J.R., 1909, 87–88).

This was the project he worked on until the end of his life.

The first appreciable presence of federalist ideas in Great Britain is connected to the problems posed by the decline of the Empire. Two political movements, composed of intellectuals and political figures (the Imperial Federation League and the Round Table Movement) were formed between the end of the 19th century and the beginning of the 20th century; they were proposing the reinforcement of the unity of the British Empire in the prospect of its transformation into a federation, seen as a remedy to the decline of Great Britain's world role. More precisely, the objective was to award to a federal government the powers relating to defence and foreign policy, and the financial resources necessary to pursue those policies, and to create a responsibility relationship between the government and a Parliament elected by all the peoples of the Commonwealth, whereas the national Parliaments would continue to take care of national problems (Curtis L., ed., 1916).

On the one hand, the necessity to promote greater security and prosperity required the reinforcement of the unity of the Commonwealth, in order to allow Great Britain to keep up with the growing market integration over ever wider spaces, and to compete with the states of regional dimensions (the United States and Russia), which had leapt to the top of the world power hierarchy. On the other, nationalism, which in the 20th century has been the cause of the disintegration of all multinational Empires, and in particular of the birth of many national liberation movements of colonial peoples, highlighted the existence of radically diverging interests between the imperial powers and their dominions, that after some time would have swept over the British Empire too. However, the fact remains that the federal model was established in some regions of the Empire: Canada in 1867, Australia in 1901 and India in 1950 gave themselves federal Constitutions.

There is also to mention the contribution by John Fiske (1842–1901), an American historian who has pondered on the universal significance of the political ideas that led to the American Constitution. He pointed out how the conceptual schemes present in *The Federalist* can help us solve the biggest problem of our time, that of peace. In a series of lectures published in 1884 he argued that "from a political viewpoint" civilization means primarily the gradual substitution of a state of peace for a state of war [. . .]. But [. . .] a general diminution of warfare is rendered possible only by the union of small political groups into larger groups that are kept together by a community of interests, and can adjust their mutual relations by legal discussion without coming to blow (Fiske J, 1902, 106–107).

> He defines federalism as the principle that "contains within itself the seeds of permanent peace between nations" (*ibid.*, 134), and considers "desirable for the states of Europe to enter into a federal union as it was the states of North America" (*ibid.*, 146); he believes that "there is really no reason [. . .] why the whole of mankind should not constitute politically one huge federation" (Fiske J, 1902, 151).

The study of federal institutions led Fiske to see peace as the value these institutions are the vehicle of. Knowingly or not, he uses the word peace in the Kantian sense, that is to say, a political organization that allows for perpetual peace among states to be realized. So, he goes beyond the Founding Fathers' limited conception, which assigned to the institutions of the United States the objective to realize isolationism, which is a milder form of nationalism.

Chapter Five

The First World War, the Crisis of the National State, and the Problem of European Unity

5.1. TROTSKY'S VIEWPOINT

The first World War represents a turning point in contemporary history, the moment when the decline of the old world order, based on the predominance of the European national-states system, and the start of the new era of world politics take on a clear evidence. In this context, the federalist project tends to assume a more concrete connotation: it appears to be an alternative to the old and crumbling order of the national states.

In the 19th century, the limits of the national states had been perceived only by isolated federalist figures, like Proudhon, Frantz and Cattaneo. They had challenged the nationalist ideology pretence to present the national state as the highest form of political organization: they had denounced its authoritarian nature, the model of a closed society that eliminates every form of social, ethnic and linguistic pluralism from within itself, and the belligerent nature of that institution that represents itself not as an historical product, but as a natural entity, and considers a natural fact mankind's organization in hostile communities, divided by national hatred.

With the spread of the national principle and the first appearance of the contradiction between this formula and the growing interdependence between Europe's peoples and states, the limits of the national state began to become practical limits of the political action itself of the national governments and the political forces supporting them. The first World War highlights that contradiction. It discloses a worrying fact: the total impotence of the European political class to control the irrational forces aroused by the historical decline of the European state-system and of the liberal, democratic and socialist ideologies; to foresee, understand and avoid that terrible historical catastrophe. The political thought of that time could not allow to identify the direction of history course, that was irresistibly tending to overcome the national state, nor to set political objectives capable to solve the contradictions which the European society was entangled in. Traditional ideologies remained prisoners of institutions they were not able to change.

However, there was who, although acting inside the cultural horizon of those same ideologies, tried to draw a lesson from the new and unexpected facts that mark a turning point in the course of history, interpreting them according to new categories. Thus, a new idea begins to emerge, which ascribes to the crisis of the national state the responsibility of war, and points to a precise alternative: the United States of Europe. Of course, they are isolated voices, which, however, are the expression of the federalist component present in the liberal, democratic and socialist political currents, and which came to the surface whenever Europe was shaken by a crisis serious enough to question the very foundations of political life.

In the socialist and communist movement, there is to mention in particular Lev D. Trotsky (1879–1940), who, at the start of World War One, wrote:

> At the root of the present war there is the revolt of the productive forces brought up by capitalism against the way the national State employs them [. . .]. The old national states [. . .] are obsolete and have turned into chains for the further development of the productive forces. The war of 1914 constitutes first of all the crisis of the national state as a self-sufficient economic area [. . .]. In such historical conditions, the solution for the European proletariat cannot but imply the defence of the obsolete fatherland, which has become the main obstacle to economic progress: the mandatory task is to create a new fatherland, much more powerful and stable, the United States of Europe as a transitional phase towards the United States of the World (Trotsky L.D., 1914, 3–6).

According to Trotsky, the evolution of the mode of production, with its industrialization process and the expansion of capitalism, while it has brought about the unification of people's behaviour in spaces of national dimensions, creating the material base of national states, has increasingly intensified the relations among peoples, creating a worldwide market. This process, driving the world, become ever smaller and interdependent in its various parts, towards unification, is the factor explaining the crisis of the national state and of the European power-system. By the expression "crisis of the national State" Trotsky means that the institutions of the national state have turned from a propulsive factor into an obstacle to the productive forces' development in the modern industrial society, which, to be in a position to grow, needs wider spaces. Europe's political division was impeding the internationalization of the productive process. Therefore, the national state had terminated its progressive historical function.

The contradiction between the productive forces' tendency to spread over the embankments of national States, and the national dimensions of political power is for Trotsky the key to interpreting the first World War. The worsening of international tensions and the search for "living space" beyond its borders by Germany are nothing else but a sign of the productive forces' thrust to organize themselves on the continental plane. In other terms, Germany's expansionist policy is a way "to unite Europe by violence" (Trotsky L.D., 1974, 319, vol. 2). This means that there is no future for the national States. The alternative Europe is confronted with is between two different forms of unity: the Empire or the Federation.

The goal of the United States of Europe had been included in the theses of "The Social-Democrat," the newspaper of the Bolshevik party, later rejected by Lenin (1870–1924) in a famous article of 1915 entitled *On the Slogan for a United States of Europe* (Lenin V.I. 1964, vol. 21, 339–343), in which, however, he did not question its positive value. In fact, Lenin merely maintained that in a capitalist regime that goal would be either impossible or reactionary, and the socialist revolution was the priority objective to pursue in every country. But as he believed that the socialist revolution was imminent not only in Russia, but in the whole continent, the United States of Europe would represent its necessary crowning. Actually, for Lenin the Russian revolution was only the first stage in a more general revolutionary process, originated by the crisis of capitalism and bound to extend itself to the whole world.

Once again in 1923, Trotsky succeeded in having the communist International adopt a resolution calling again for the United States of Europe, when the occupation of the Ruhr dramatically put forward the issue of the Franco-German rivalry, with the dangers that its outbreak was implying for the European balance and for the hope of a revolution in Germany and its eventual extension to the rest of Europe, that had been revived for the last time. But it was dropped with Stalin, who exiled and wanted Trotsky murdered. Thus, the principle of building socialism in one country prevailed.

Trotsky's theory of a "permanent revolution," although based on an insubstantial assumption, namely the possibility of a proletarian revolution in Europe, is characterized by his keen awareness that socialism could not survive in one country without degenerating.

The essence of our epoch lies in this,—he wrote in 1929—that the productive forces have definitively outgrown the framework of the national state and have assumed primarily in America and Europe partly continental, partly world proportions. The imperialist war grew out of the contradiction between the productive forces and national boundaries. And the Versailles peace which terminated the war has aggravated this contradiction still further. In other words: thanks to the development of the productive forces, capitalism has long ago been unable to exist in a single country. But socialism can and will base itself on far more developed productive forces, otherwise socialism would represent not progress but regression with respect to capitalism" (Trotsky L.D., 1975, 356, vol. 1).

It is condemned to degenerate in one country, and may develop only in a regional dimension and establish itself permanently in a world federation. The horrors of Stalinism will prove the correctness of this opinion. However, the building of socialism in one country had no alternatives. Stripped of polemic exaggerations, Stalin's design was taking note of the failure of the prospect to extend the socialist revolution to Europe and wanted to show that the Soviet Union had sufficient resources to be able to survive in a hostile world, counting only on its own forces. Stalin understood that, thanks to its size, the USSR could aspire to fill the gap with the rest of Europe through forced industrialization and climb to the top of the world power hierarchy. The choice of nationalism allowed the USSR to become the big power that contributed in a decisive measure to the defeat of Nazi Germany, and will rule, together with the USA, the world destiny in the second post-war period.

Trotsky's great merit is to have contributed to introduce in political culture the notion of crisis of the national state and to base on it a comprehensive historical analysis on the contemporary world. He has described a fundamental aspect of the crisis of the national state (*the incompatibility between the dimensions of that type of state and the development of productive forces*) and has remarked the fact that the overcoming of the national state was the central problem of our time, which raises the issue of creating economic spaces and hence the necessity of organizing the state over territories of dimensions as great as entire world regions. The formula of the United States of Europe is precisely the political expression of the idea that socialism is impossible in one country.

The limit of his historical vision is to consider the crisis of the national state as an aspect of a deeper phenomenon: the crisis of capitalism, compelled to transform itself in imperialism in order to have the possibility to develop beyond its national borders. All Marxist writers of the time, from Lenin to Rosa Luxemburg, consider imperialism and war as manifestations of the insoluble contradictions of capitalism in the phase of its full development and its imminent collapse. Actually, the conflicts generated by capitalism do not produce any war in the United States, because the power to declare war has been transferred from the federated states to the federal government, and all conflicts can be settled before a court, whilst Europe has been torn by the world wars because its political organization was based on the principle of unlimited national sovereignty. While Trotsky continued for all his life to wait for the collapse of capitalism and the socialist revolution, in Europe fascism established itself. His ideology is just a variant of the theory of imperialism as the supreme phase of capitalism. He continues to see the main front of political struggle in the conflict between capitalism and socialism. Therefore, he indicates in an internal feature of the state, that is, in a particular organizational type of the economic system, the root cause of war, and believes that the automatic consequence of the socialist revolution, in Europe first and then in the whole world, will be peace.

In sum, one element of Trotsky's interpretation of the world war has to be corrected to make it consistent with the materialistic conception of history. The term "capitalism" (a "superstructure," that is, an organizational form of economy) has to be substituted with the expression "industrial mode of production" (the "structure," that is, the mode of production). The confusion between historical materialism and economy, which has its roots in the works by Marx and Engels, allows us to explain some inconsistencies in the Marxism-inspired interpretations of imperialism. In fact, at the root of the world war there is the industrial mode of production in its phase of internationalization of the production process, and not capitalism.

On the other hand, it would be useless to look in Trotsky's works for any reflection on the institutional nature of the formula of the United States of Europe. According to the Marxist approach, Trotsky considered political institutions as mere superstructures and underestimated the relative autonomy that the state and the world system of states have in determining the course of history. As a consequence, the distinction between federation and confederation, that is, between a union of states contemplating and a union of states not contemplating transfers of sovereignty, of such importance for the theory of political institutions, is totally ignored.

5.2 THE FEDERALIST COMPONENT IN THE RUSSIAN REVOLUTION AND SOCIALISM IN ONE COUNTRY

Also in the Russian Revolution, as in the French Revolution, a federalist component may be found. Although a systematic reconstruction in this direction has not been attempted yet, it is undeniable that in the Russian Revolution there has been the presence of the cosmopolitan aspect of federalism, that is to say the aim of peace and universal solidarity among men and the fight against the unequal distribution of power and wealth in the world, as well as the community aspect of federalism, that is to say the claim for a political and economic democracy based on self-ruling of basic organizations with a territorial (communes) and functional (factory councils and agricultural cooperatives) character.

On the one hand, the cosmopolitan values of the French Revolution, run over by the prevailing national egoisms, were resumed by the Russian Revolution. We have seen that Trotsky had launched the slogan of the United States of Europe, seen as a stage on the road to the world federation, which had been accepted both by the Russian social-democratic party and by the communist International. In addition, he had forecast that socialism, if it remained confined in one country, would be condemned to defeat, and therefore it should spread over the European continent in order to open the way to its universal establishment. On the other, in the system of the *Soviets* the requirement emerged to decentralize power and to have autonomy in political and economic management against the burocratic and centralizing tendencies of the state. The Russian experience of local councils represents the outline of some elements of a federal organization, foreshadowed in Proudhon's thought and present in the Russian cultural tradition through the federalist component in Bakunin's work. As an immediate witness, Georges Gurvitch (1894–1965) wrote:

> The first Russian Soviets have been organized by Proudhonians [. . .]. They could not derive from Marx the idea of the Revolution through the base *Soviets*, because it is an essentially, exclusively Proudhonian idea. As I am one of the organizers of the Russian *Soviets* of 1917, I can speak of them with a full knowledge of the facts (Gurvitch G., 1967, 96).

The federal arrangement of the Constitution of the Soviet Union is more the result of a necessity than of a choice of principle. Lenin inspired his political vision to two ideas (that of national self-determination and that of democratic centralism), which not only were barring the prospect of federalism, but were also incompatible with keeping Russia's multinational structure. He counted on the alliance between the social-democratic party and the national movement, seen as a powerful factor of disintegration of the Empire, and took a stand for self-determination of all peoples up to secession and against any form of forced union, a principle that will be proclaimed in the *Declaration of the rights of the peoples of Russia* of November 15, 1917. In *State and Revolution* Lenin stated he shared Marx's and Engel's opinions, that the political organization most in accordance with the interests of the working class is the unitary state, based on the principle of democratic centralism, which allows to break feudal particularism and develops a modern industrial society. Federal institutions are considered a necessary and progressive solution only in two historical circumstances: a state of very large dimensions, like the United States, and a multinational state, like the United Kingdom. And even in these cases the federal solution is seen as a transitional form on the road to a centralized republic (Lenin V. I., 1964, 427–430, vol. 25). On 28 March 1917 Stalin (1879–1953) published in the *Pravda* an article with a telling title, *Against Federalism*, in which he maintained the same theses and stated: "In Russia it would be unwise to work for federation, which is doomed by the very realities of life to disappear" (Stalin J., 27, vol. 3).

Only after the October Revolution did the state's federal organization impose itself as a necessity, because it was offering a formula by which the secessionist tendencies could be reined in through the concession of autonomy to all the peoples. The *Declaration of Rights of the Working and Exploited People*, written by Lenin, approved by the Central Committee of the Bolshevik Party in January 1918 and included in the Russian Constitution, is the document marking the line change. It proclaims the Russian Soviet Republic "a federation of national Soviet Republics" (Lenin V. I., 1964, 423, vol. 26). Actually, the organization of the Russian state was not the example of a federal regime, but simply of administrative decentralization.

The Bolsheviks wanted to set up egalitarian relations between the Russian nation and the non-Russian nations. Convinced that the workers' unity would have allowed them to avoid disaggregating the state's unity, they had applied to the entire territory of the Czars' Empire the principle of the independence of every people, to whom they had recognized the right of self-determination up to secession and to creating an independent state. Poland, Finland, the Baltic states declared their independence, but did not show any willingness to join the Soviet state. Other nations were ready to exercise their right to secession. The unity of the peoples which had freed themselves from the Czarist oppression was at risk of shattering. The socialist character of the forces that had knocked down the power of the Czars had proved inadequate to keep political unity of all the territories that were part of the Empire. And it was clearer and clearer that a world revolution was not imminent. Therefore, the consolidation of the Soviet state was indispensable for making its survival possible in a world of hostile states. Thus, the reality of force relations, that governs international politics, imposed itself also in the countries where the Russian Revolution had won: the Red Army's military intervention in Georgia in 1921, where independence had been declared by a Menshevik government, put an end to the movement of national independence.

Only at this point was the federal formula recognized as the only one capable to aggregate the nations that had freed themselves from the Czarist oppression in a single political frame and to assure at the same time their independence. That choice gave birth to the Constitution of the USSR in 1924, which is the result of a clash between Lenin, who wanted a federation of equal Republics, and Stalin, who proposed the concession of autonomy to the various national groups and their inclusion in the Russian Soviet Republic.

Formally Lenin's position prevailed. Although the USSR Constitution did not define itself as federal, it was the result of an agreement between sovereign states, whose powers were limited only in the matters explicitly mentioned in the Constitution, and to the Soviet Republics the right to secession, was even recognized. However, there remained the reality of the disparity between Russia and the other national groups.

The single-party dictatorship allowed Stalin to pursue power centralization and to consolidate the greater-Russian hegemony over the other nations of the USSR. The federal Constitution was thought of by its authors as a transitional phase towards complete union. Almost one century on, it is possible to observe that, despite Stalin's brutal centralizing policy, national realities have not been erased. Indeed, they show an extraordinary vitality. A proof of the validity of the federal political formula in compounding the principles of unity and diversity in multi-national societies and over territories of vast dimensions may be the Russian Constitution of 1993, which has again opened the road to a reorganization of institutions in a federal sense.

The Russian Revolution has modified the course of world history by thrusting in the fracture of a radical opposition to the capitalist system. This has been made possible by the presence in the Soviet Union of the necessary political conditions (political structure and dimensions) for guaranteeing the development of the productive forces and the state's international autonomy, whilst in the states of central and western Europe the workers' movement, isolated and choked within its narrow national borders, suffered the spread of fascist totalitarianism. The peaceful and communitarian ideals of federalism, which had emerged in the French Revolution and never disappeared from the underground current of history, surfaced again during the Russian Revolution, but did not find a fertile ground for their realization. Still today they are just anticipations of a society to come. The fact is that such revolutions, as the expression defining them says, have taken place in one country, whereas revolution is worldwide and universal.

The authoritarian and imperialistic character taken by the Soviet Union highlights how the Russian Revolution, despite its universal message of emancipation, did not succeed in solving the problems posed by the establishment of the national state, namely the integral realization of the principle of popular sovereignty and solidarity among peoples. The Russian Revolution's degeneration shows that even Marxism had to come to terms with the *raison d'état*. Which means that what it was negating in theory it had to accept later in practice (it is not possible to assert the values against power relations, which dominate world politics, unless one conforms himself to the laws which such relations obey). It is not surprising then, for those who let themselves be guided by the category of *raison d'état*, that socialism could endure in one country of gigantic dimensions, able to defend its independence against the encirclement of an hostile world. The leading state of the socialist experience subordinated to its own national interest that of international socialism and world revolution. In its struggle for survival it was forced to abandon the *soviets* system, the perspective of the fading away of the state and the assertion of the communist society and tried by any means (including military occupation) to subdue to its *raison d'état* the various components of the international communist movement. In addition to this international factor, other two domestic factors contributed to power centralization: the frightful backwardness of the Soviet Union, where there was no democratic tradition and the material and cultural conditions had not been reached yet for a democratic participation of the great masses in the political life; and secondly the urgent need for a quick industrialization, which implied forced accumulation and the compression of consumption.

5.3 EINAUDI 'S STANDPOINT

The peculiar similarity of Trotsky's and Einaudi's (1874–1961) positions on the first World War has remained unnoticed. Although they started from so distant political and cultural experiences that one must exclude there has ever been between the two figures any form of intellectual dialogue, they come to a largely convergent interpretation of that war and launch an appeal for the United States of Europe. This fact, however surprising, may be explained considering that, confronted with the new trends in history contemporary history, both of them tried to advance on a new road.

Einaudi, in two articles published in *Il Corriere della Sera* in 1918, found the root of the crisis of the national state, along the same line of Trotsky's interpretation, in the strong increase of economic interdependence.

What are—he asked himself—the treaties on the post, on health, on railroads, on industrial and intellectual property, on brands, other than a relinquishment of the full and absolute sovereignty of individual states, other than a substantial, if masked, abdication by the Parliaments of their right to make laws at their will within the boundaries of their state territory? (Einaudi L., 33–34).

Here is the root of the decline of national sovereignty ("Parliaments have rapidly turned into registration bureaus," he says).

When matters subject to discussion and deliberation have an international nature, they cannot be discussed and decided by municipal Parliaments. Above the states, become small, almost as big counties, and their deliberating bodies, there must form, there have been ideally constituted already, larger states, government bodies different from the normal ones (Einaudi L., 34).

Exactly like Trotsky, Einaudi defines war as a sign of the need of Europe's unity: "The present war is the condemnation of European unity imposed by force by a bold Empire; but it is also the bloody effort to frame a political form of a higher order" (Einaudi L., 27). He too considers European unity as a stage on the road to world unity: "To the United States of America there should be opposed or associated the United States of Europe, awaiting the birth in a later moment of human civilization of the United States of the world" (Einaudi L., 19). But, unlike Trotsky, he is aware of the institutional innovation brought by the Philadelphia Convention, which marked the birth of the federation. As the United States of America constituted themselves "transforming a shadow, an unreal society of nations ready to split and fight each other, into a single state of a higher order than the 13 confederated states" (Einaudi L., 26), likewise in the United States of Europe the nations will guarantee "to themselves as parts of a higher state body a real security against the attempts at hegemony which, in the present international anarchy, the stronger state is invincibly driven at by the ruinous dogma of absolute sovereignty" (Einaudi L., 36).

With regard to Einaudi's analysis, the most significant study in Giovanni Agnelli's (1866–1945) and Attilio Cabiati's (1872–1950) book *European Federation or League of Nations?* (1918) consists in their explicit reception of the theory of *raison d'état*. They mention Heinrich von Treitschke (1834–1896), one of the most representative figures of the school of the power-state, to assert the thesis that

> the clash [. . .] between the theoretical right of small nations to independent statehood and the natural tendency of large political masses to absorb smaller masses into their orbit, in order to give the whole a richer and more uniform framework and life. [They state that] both principles are founded on a basis of truth; but the national solution has not enabled them to coexist peacefully [And they conclude that] the absorption of small states into the bigger and stronger organisms that surround them has on the whole been to the advantage of human society (Agnelli G. and Cabiati A., 28).

However, accepting the principles of the *raison d'état* does not represent an obstacle to a polemic attitude towards a culture that was critically adhering to the nationalist viewpoint, and that considered the division of the world in sovereign states as a natural and eternal reality. On the wake of the federalist thinking tradition dating back to Hamilton and Kant, they consider the *raison d'état* as an historically transitory reality, bound to be surpassed by the progressive extension of federal institutions and by the ensuing pacification process between ever wider human groups. Thus, they detach themselves from the pacifist and internationalist version of federalism, the trend prevailing till then in the movement for peace and European unity, but defeated in the world war.

In the federalist tradition, Einaudi believes that state sovereignty is the ultimate cause of war. Therefore, peace cannot be but the result of unity of the states under a Constitution giving birth to a democratic government, granted the necessary powers to forbid and avert the use of force in the relations among states. What is peculiar to the federalist theory is that the cause of war is not ascribed to certain internal structures of the state (for example, the capitalist system, as maintained by the Marxist theory), but to the mere division of the world in sovereign states, as a consequence of which, whatever the political regime and productive system, it must yield to the law of force to defend its independence. If international anarchy is a permanent feature of the international political system and can only be overcome by a world federation, it is made worse by what Einaudi calls "the dogma of State sovereignty," that is to say the national principle. It finds its highest expression in the power

> to declare war and to sign peace. From that attribute derive all the other prerogatives of the sovereign and perfect state: to have the authority, it alone, to exact absolute obedience by its citizens, to levy armies and collect taxes, to do justice without being subject to any court placed above it, to make mandatory laws for all moral bodies and physical persons living on its national territory, to negate independent sovereignty to any body, like the Church, on its territory, to sign treaties with other sovereign states and to repeal them. [In addition], the fixed idea [. . .] of sovereignty cannot exist politically and militarily unless it does not exist economically. The commercially closed-in State is not just an ideological abstract idea of the philosopher Fichte. It must become a reality, if the German state wants to be truly sovereign and independent. [That principle, that is used to justify power centralization and economic self-sufficiency, turns national states into hostile and war-leaning groups.] The chosen states, like the German had been convinced to be by the pan-Germanic literature, use that dogma as a very sharp instrument for conquest and supremacy, which cannot be fully satisfied but when it becomes worldwide (Einaudi, 29–31).

In essence, the fusion of state and nation was tending to suppress all the spontaneous ties that men had always had to political, social and religious institutions, smaller or bigger than the nation, in order to avoid that other ties could make weaker the absolute loyalty the state was exacting from its citizens and to place at the central government's service the material and ideal resources of the country, thus making possible a swift mobilization in case of war. In an era when industrial revolution was increasing the number and intensity of the relations between individuals of different states, the national state was trying to eliminate the domestic and international restraints that had regulated the clashes among states when they were founded on the dynastic principle, by spreading the ideological conviction that nations are absolutely different human groups, founded on irreconcilable principles. Germany's national unification is the historical event that brings about the crisis of the European power system. Germany soon established itself as the strongest power in the continent, and entered into conflict with Great Britain. For countering its trading and naval predominance it adopted a protectionist system and built up a navy. This policy, which upset Great Britain's balancing role on the European continent, made harsher the tensions in Europe, disintegrated the international order and made the world war inevitable.

Einaudi then had the perception of another fundamental aspect of the crisis of the national State: *the incompatibility between national state and the international order*. "The dogma of state sovereignty—he wrote—is in irremediable contrast with the idea of the League of Nations" (Einaudi, 30). Thus, if the division of Europe in sovereign states has been the general cause of war, that is a situation that affects both the cold war and the warred war, or, to use Kant's language, the truce and the war. The internationalization of the productive process and the crisis of the European balance of power are two factors that let Einaudi explain the specific causes of the world war. The federalist theory of war and peace, thus, have let Einaudi overcome the limits of Trotsky's conception both with regard to the identification of the ultimate cause of war, and with regard to the means to build peace.

5.4 THE CRITICISM OF THE LIMITS OF INTERNATIONALISM: THE LEAGUE OF NATIONS AND THE WORKERS' INTERNATIONALS

After the first World War it was quite clear that the European power system was no longer capable to find in itself the resources necessary for solving its own problems. Germany's defeat was determined by the overwhelming weight of the United States, as it will be the United States again, with the Soviet Union, that will give a decisive contribution to the defeat of Hitler's Germany. In fact, the United States coming into the first World War marks the fading of the European system and the start of the era of world politics.

What Wilson's (1856–1924) and Lenin's visions have in common is their refusal to accept the European balance as the context in which to rebuild the international order of the first post-war period. Their viewpoint is more advanced because they adopted a world perspective, they acknowledged a real change in the force relations among states, namely the tendency of the power to make decisions in the international plane to move out of Europe and the emergence of a world system of states whose pillars should have been the United States and the Soviet Union.

The limit of their vision is in having promoted the principle of peoples' self-determination, in not having been able to go beyond an idea of international policy based on the primacy of the sovereign states. Wilson's appeal for the creation of a League of Nations and Lenin's for a world revolution, imbued as they were with idealism and utopia, still were gathering some essential aspects of the new political reality. First of all, they were addressing themselves to all peoples on Earth, underlining thus the fact that in the era of democracy and nationalism a growing involvement of public opinion in international politics was necessary. Secondly, they believed that the world could not live in peace until it was divided between communism and democracy. One day, one of the two principles would end up prevailing. It is an anticipation of the worldwide conflict between the Russian and the American super-powers that in the second post-war period will take on the aspect of an ideological clash between communism and democracy, while the victory of each super-power over its rival will be portrayed as unification of the world and realization of universal peace. So, the first World War showed that Europe's organization in national States was utterly incompatible not only with international balance, but also with the development of productive forces. Thus the problem arose of reorganizing the world according to new formulas: Wilson proposed the League of Nations, and Lenin the communist International.

With the first World War federalism took on a clearer theoretical stance and sharply marked its difference from internationalism and from the vague pacifist ideas of international solidarity it was generally confused with. To the problem of how to govern the internationalization of political, economic and social life, and the crisis of the European power balance, two different solutions emerge. The first is internationalism, which advocates the method of international co-operation, also through the creation of international organizations, either governmental (as the League of Nations) or non-governmental (as the workers' Internationals), but without questioning national sovereignty. The second is federalism, whose objective is to overcome the diplomatic-intergovernmental method in the perspective of creating a truly democratic government above the States, provided with the powers necessary to eliminate violence from international politics.

Federalism is not just one of the possible approaches to controlling international politics; it is also a standpoint that allows one to highlight the limits of internationalism and, in particular, of solutions such as the workers' Internationals or the League of Nations. The latter is the expression of an awareness and a need partly shared by the federalist thought: that the problem of peace cannot be solved by simply transforming the political or economic structures of individual states, and therefore it is necessary to invent new forms of international organization.

In 1916 Herbert George Wells (1866–1946) wrote: "My reason insists on the inevitableness and necessity of this ultimate reconciliation [between the Allied and German peoples]. I will do no more than I must to injure Germany further, and I will do all that I can to restore the unity of mankind" (Wells H. G., 1916, 294). He argued against Wilson's "obsession by the idea of the sovereignty of 'nationalities' and his incapacity to think out what he meant by a nationality" (Wells H. G., 1929, 82). This would have contributed to fragment the world and add a new factor of international tensions and war, unless the new national states born out of the dissolution of the big Empires would associate themselves in "a federal Union on the model of the United States and Switzerland" (Wells H. G., 1916, 294). In 1916, together with George Grey (1862–1922), James Bryce (1862–1933), Lionel Curtis (1872–1955) and others he constituted the League for Free Nations Association, which in 1918 promoted the publication of a pamphlet, *The Idea of a League of Nations*, of which Wells is the main author. In the last page it reads:

> The League of Nations cannot be a little thing: it is either to be a great thing in the world, an overriding idea of a greater state, or nothing, [. . .] it is an idle and wasteful diplomacy, a pandering to timidities state and shams, to pretend that the World-League of Nations is not ultimately a state aiming at that ennobled individual whose city is the world" (Wells H. G., 1919, 44).

Despite the League of Nations had nothing in common with the idea of a world state, Wells continued for the whole of his life to believe that it was possible to realize the dream of a world state. Indeed, he believed that it was inevitable.

Wells believed that the novelties brought by science and technology, the revolution in communication and transport would bring about the overcoming of the world organization in sovereign states. With remarkable far-sightedness he saw that science was producing the conditions for a world state. Science creates the technologies that reduce distances and unify humankind. At the same time it creates the weapons that threaten to destroy the world. In a novel of 1914, *The World Set Free, A Story of Mankind*, Wells imagined the end of civilization in a war fought with nuclear weapons. However, faced with the difficulty of thinking of the world federation in the era of world wars, in the era when democracy had given way to nationalism, Wells was fascinated by the myth of technocracy. He, who considered himself a scientist, imagined that an elite of scientists, technicians, industrialists, bankers, writers could constitute themselves in a kind of open secret-society and operate for building the world state, simply ignoring the national states and considering obsolete the world of politics (Wells, H.G., 1928).

In practice, however, the League of Nations was unable to control international disorder and guarantee peace, as Einaudi showed since 1918. In fact, its structure was conceived as "a kind of perpetual alliance or confederation of States" in which "the allied or confederated states remained fully sovereign and independent," and not as "a true super-state provided with direct sovereignty over the citizens of the various states" (Einaudi L., 20). Aware of the distinction between federation and confederation, Einaudi formulated a precise judgement on the nature of the League of Nations, and gave a warning to those who were under the illusion that peace can be attained without questioning national sovereignty. "Do we want to fight for a name or for a real thing?" he wanders. And adds: "The efforts made for creating a society of nations that continue to be sovereign would create just nothing, the unthinkable, they would only increase and poison the reasons for discord and war" (Einaudi, 22–23). Whereas the European ruling class was expecting from the Treaty of Versailles, which had generalized the national principle and instituted the League of Nations, the start of an era of peace, Einaudi made the forecast, fully confirmed by history, that the divisions and conflicts among European states will become even harsher.

In fact, after the war the United States withdrew into its traditional isolation, the Soviet Union retired into itself in an effort to create a modern industrial society, and Europe was left a prey to nationalism. The consequence of the new European order born out of the Treaty of Versailles was that Europe, with its mosaic of small states fighting each other, was run over by the growing international anarchy, and democracy, choked in too narrow spaces, was condemned to die of suffocation. The contradictions caused by not having overcome national sovereignties will come back in a more serious form, because history continually presents back again the problems people fail to dominate theoretically and solve practically. Thus, the preconditions were set for fascism and nazism, for the second World War and for the final collapse of the European system of states.

The federalist perspective also allows us to see the limits of the workers' Internationals and to establish a relationship between the disintegration of those organizations and the *raison d'état* and war. In fact, in the decisive time of war, national solidarity always prevails over the ties linking the working classes the world over. The Franco-Prussian war spread nationalist sentiments within the warring countries and inflicted a deadly blow on the First International. The first World War broke up the alliance between the working classes in the Second International, and brought about the alliance of the working classes of the various States with their national middle classes and against the proletariat of the other countries. And still is the war (the second World War) the element explaining the dissolution of the Third International. The Soviet Union's alliance with the biggest countries of the western world required the cessation of what was the organ of world revolution, in the name of a collaboration imposed by the necessity to defeat Nazi Germany and its allies. The survival of Comintern had thus become incompatible with the objectives imposed by the Soviet Union's *raison d'état*.

What happened to the Internationals may illustrate an often-unnoticed relationship between internationalism and international anarchy. The impotence shown by the Internationals in regard to war was not accidental, but the expression of a structural tendency. International relations are dominated by a mechanism that irresistibly tends, especially in the most critical stages of the crisis of the international political system like wars are, to divide the workers' international movement and to make national solidarity prevail, even between rival classes, over international class-solidarity. This mechanism is international anarchy.

International socialism cannot stand international anarchy—Barbara Wootton (1897–1988) wrote commenting on the failure of the Second International. The claims of national security, if not of rampant nationalism, are too strong. As long as there is no machinery other than war to deal with political gangsters, the socialist is faced with an intolerable dilemma. Either he must take up arms against his comrades, or he must lie down before to aggression. He has generally chosen the former alternative. And socialism as an international movement is in ruins. [While international socialism is obliged to yield to international anarchy, it can only succeed within a state]: Experience has shown that it is possible to build Trade Unions that are capable of concerted action over vast geographical areas, provided that they do not extend beyond the boundaries of independent states (Wootton B., 277 and 289).

The cause of the failure of socialist internationalism, and of any other form of internationalism, lies in the objective structure of the political international system. The organization of political power, of the struggle among political parties and among social forces, of the citizens' consent in the national arena, that is to say the inertia of national institutions, has prevented the mechanisms of international society, left thus far to diplomatic and military clashes among states not regulated by laws, from opening up to the control by the people and the workers. Democratic procedures for making political decisions and for organizing the masses stop at the state border. Individuals, singly or organized in political parties or unions, do not have any instrument of political action at their disposal beyond their national borders, except the foreign policy procedures at the top. Still today the institutions through which democratic participation takes place make it possible to operate in one's own country only. As a consequence, only if the problem, neglected by internationalism, of how to limit the exclusive national sovereignty, the ultimate cause of power politics and war, is solved, will it become possible to subject international politics to the same rules domestic politics obeys.

Chapter Six

English Constitutional Federalism and the Crisis of the European System of States between the World Wars

The crisis of the national State, which broke out with the first World War, made possible the beginning of the contemporary advocating the European Union. In the first place, there is to mention *Paneuropa*, a movement constituted in Vienna in 1923 on the initiative of Richard Coudenhove-Kalergi (1894–1973) and grown mostly on the European continent. This movement gained a hearing from many heads of state and government or ministers (such as Stresemann (1878–1929), Briand (1862–1932), Churchill (1874–1965), Beneš (1884–1948), Masaryk (1850–1937) and Mussolini (1883–1945)), political leaders, diplomats, and intellectuals, an élite circle without a democratic base. Coudenhove's goal was the re-establishment of the Habsburg empire through a confederation stretching out on the whole of Europe with Vienna as its capital. This movement was the inspirer of a project for European Union presented by Aristide Briand to the League of Nations in 1929, but without success.

History was barring the way to the pan-European idea. The European power system, despite its deep decline, was continuing to play a hegemonic world role thanks to the isolationism of the United States and the Soviet Union. The problem of European unity could only be posed in terms of a co-operation among states with the aim to counter the great powers at the sides of the European system, which will form the two poles of the world system of states, and to let them keep their colonial Empires. In fact, Briand's project was taking the utmost care not to scratch state sovereignty; it had a confederal, not a federal character. But the opposition of Great Britain, loyal to its political tradition aimed at countering any attempt to unify the continent, and later Adolf Hitler's (1889–1945) coming to power in Germany caused the collapse of the fragile diplomatic construction whose purpose was to give

80

birth to an embryo of European organization, based on an agreement between Briand and Stresemann.

Coudenhove-Kalergi's political ideas reflect in some way the limits of the historical context he lived in. On the one hand, he lucidly defined the historical terms of the European problem: "Will it be possible for Europe, in its state of political and economic disunity, to preserve its peace and independence in the face of the growing strength of the extra-European world powers—or will Europe's preservation, be conditional upon the formation of a federation?" (Coudenhove-Kalergi R., 95). On the other, however, the practical obstacles hindering European unification may explain the rough and imprecise nature of his project of a European federation, which, together with democratic states, was including also fascist Italy.

A quite greater relevance has the Federal Union movement (Mayne R., Pinder J., Roberts J.) constituted in 1939 in Great Britain, a particularly favourable observation point for studying the decline of the European system of states. The federalist component of this political culture had important theoretical developments first in the context of the crisis of the national state and after the second World War, when some proposals emerged, as alternatives to the crisis, of a federation of European (or western world) democracies, seen as a stage towards a world federation. The proposal of a federation among the fifteen democracies of North America, Europe and the Commonwealth was formulated by an American journalist, Clarence Streit (1896–1986), a correspondent from 1929 to 1939 of the *New York Times* from Geneva, where he was present at the collapse of the League of Nations and noted its limits, that he described in the book *Union Now* (1939).

The success of this book favoured the spreading of federalist ideas and the formation of the British federalist movement, and of a similar movement in the United States. It is uncertain how many members joined Federal Union in the United Kingdom—estimates vary between ten and sixty thousand: by 1940 there were no fewer than 253 local branches. The movement was supported by so many distinguished people that Mayne and Pinder are able to claim that "the establishment" gave it its backing (Mayne R., Pinder J., Roberts J., 19). Moreover, the fact that 100,000 copies of William B. Curry's *The Case for Federal Union* (1939) were sold after the outbreak of war shows the extraordinary impact that the movement had on British public opinion. Federal Union represents a milestone in the history of federalism: the first example of a federalist movement made up of a group of active members capable of exerting an influence on political, intellectual and social circles and public opinion, organized over the territory with local branches and a newsletter. This organizational model is not substantially different from that applied by post-war federalist movements. Moreover, it is worth recalling that a referendum on Streit's project, promoted in August 1942 by the magazine *Fortune*, got ten million positive answers in the United States.

The theoretical importance of the Anglo-Saxon federalism consists in having defined more precisely, in relation to the problems posed by the crisis of the European system, the principles of federalism drawn by Kant and Hamilton. In fact, the European system was a full-fledged system of national states, the expression of the deepest political division of mankind, and of the tightest power centralization that modern history had ever known. However, whereas for those two authors federalism consists in transcending a group of sovereign states with a democratic structure, the political program of the Anglo-Saxon federalists focuses on transcending historically consolidated nations and asserting the illegitimacy of the national state.

Lord Lothian (Philip Kerr) (1882–1940) studied in depth and developed Kant's conception of history as the realization of peace through the progressive elimination of violence in all social relations. The stages at the extremes of this process are, according to Kant: the constitution of states, that allowed men to leave the state of nature, and their union in a universal federation, that will allow mankind to leave the state of war. Lothian, analysing in depth the institutional mechanisms that allow the pacification process among peoples to be extended, found three phases in that process that coincide with the progressive enlargement of the dimensions of the democratic government.

> Greek civilization—he wrote—was developed mainly in the city states of Greece. But the Greeks could not rise above a city patriotism and the Athenians, who thought that public affairs should be directly controlled by all the citizens, did not believe that a democratic community could be larger than the number of free citizens who could hear the voice of a single orator. Because Greece was unable to evolve a national patriotism or the representative institutions appropriate to it, it was in due time overwhelmed by the totalitarian state of Macedon. [. . .] The missing representative system was developed under the Plantagenets in England and made possible the combination of the reign of law with the principle that government must be with the consent of the governed, which is the foundation of the Parliamentary system and made possible democracy on a national scale. The Americans, confronted with the problem of uniting states which, in separating from Great Britain, had already established their own sovereignty, discovered the federal principle whereby the powers and functions of government were divided between states and commonwealth. This discovery made possible the development of a system of federal union which combined complete state autonomy with democratically controlled reign of law on a continental scale (Lord Lothian, 1990, *The Ending of Armageddon*, 12–13).

Lord Lothian thoroughly examined the significance of the connection, already found by Kant, between peace and the democratic character of the structure of the states accepting the federative pact between them: the stages in the establishment of peace are the stages in the enlargement of the democratic government, from the city to the nation, and to the federal union of nations. The institutions that have made this historical evolution possible are: assembly democracy, representative democracy and federal democracy. The latter is potentially in a position to found peace on a universal democratic order.

In a booklet with the telling title *Pacifism is not Enough* (1935) Lord Lothian precisely described the federalist theory on the nature of war and peace, in relation to the problems of contemporary society. We find there three propositions:

> The first is that war is inherent and cannot be prevented in a world of sovereign states. The second is that the League of Nations and the Kellogg Pact, however valuable they may be valid as intermediate educative steps, cannot end war and preserve civilization or peace. The third is that peace, in the political sense of the word, that is, the ending of war, can only be established by bringing the whole world under the reign of law, through the creation of a world state, and that until we succeed in creating a federal commonwealth of nations, which need not, at the start, embrace the whole earth, we shall not have laid even the foundation for the ending of the institution of war upon earth (Lord Lothian, 1990 *Pacifism is not Enough nor Patriotism Either*, 223–224).

The federalist theory distinguishes itself from the current theories of international relations in that it explains international politics with categories different from the ones used for domestic politics. It employs the category of international anarchy, because there has never been on the international plane the power-concentration process that has taken place within the states, and it defines as violence-leaning and non-juridical the specific character of the relations among states. Thus, the federalist theory ascribes war and international tensions not to certain features of the states' structure (authoritarian character of governments or capitalist character of the economic system), but to international anarchy, even if it does not negate the mutual influence of the states' internal structure on international politics. Moreover, peace is not simply a negative situation (the absence of war), but a positive situation (the state), an institution that makes it possible to solve the political, economic and social problems through laws and courts. Thus, it is the result of a specific struggle whose objective is to create a democratic power above the states. Therefore, it is an illusion to expect peace from international cooperation or from the state's transformation in a liberal, democratic or socialist sense.

Quite noticeable is his criticism of the theory, still dominant today, that ascribes war to capitalism. Lord Lothian writes:

> It is perfectly true that both the capitalists and the trade unions are largely responsible for ever-mounting tariffs, and endeavour to enlist the support of Foreign Officers in their search for foreign markets or to protect their interests abroad, or their standard of living at home—all of which adds to international tension. It is perfectly true that certain armaments manufacturers and certain newspapers have fomented international suspicion as a method of getting profitable orders or circulation for themselves. But these things are the consequences and not the cause of the division of the world into sixty sovereign states. The division of the world into state sovereignties long antedated modern capitalism. Capitalism does not cause war inside the state. Nor would it produce war inside a federation of nations. It is the division of humanity into sovereign states which disturbs the pacific functioning of capitalism as an international force and causes war, not capitalism which is the cause of the division of the world into an anarchy of sovereign states.

> Can socialism remedy these evils? Only if it creates a federal commonwealth of nations [. . .]. Sixty sovereign socialist states can no more be self-supporting than can sixty capitalist states. Only Russia and the United States, by tremendous efforts, might make themselves self-contained under either system. Yet it is going to be no more easy for sixty sovereign socialist states to agree upon what each is to produce for and take from the other, with the tremendous consequences involved on the internal standard of living and the distribution of labour and employment in each, than it is for sixty capitalist states to arrange barter systems or mutually beneficial tariff systems. Their relations might even become more violent because every economic act would be an act of state, which might bring ruin or starvation to other states. The root of our economic as of our political troubles is the division of the world into sovereign states. Neither capitalism nor socialism can function until this anarchy is overcome (Lord Lothian, 1990, *Pacifism is not Enough nor Patriotism Either*, 226–227).

Although recognizing the importance of economic factors in the origin of international conflicts, Lord Lothian observes that within states economic conflicts do not have war as their outcome. Instead, international economic conflicts are ultimately solved by war because there does not exist above the states a power capable to solve them with the instruments of law. The ultimate cause of war has a political nature: it is the world's division in sovereign states. Moreover, he observes that socialism is not by itself capable to eliminate international conflicts. Indeed, in a world of socialist states those conflicts would tend to become worse, because the state property of production means tends to politicize international trading relations and to increase the reasons of friction among states.

The fundamental contradiction of our time is not the one that opposes capitalism and socialism within national states, but that between nationalism and federalism. The national state, whatever its political regime and its economic system, tends to hinder the development of productive forces and it is a dragging factor for the historical process, which is pushing towards the formation of states of regional dimensions. Instead, Soviet socialism and American capitalism have proved to be evolutionary experiences because, expressing themselves in a regional-state context, as required by the modern conditions of industrial production and military technology necessary to maintain economic development and political independence, they have been able to develop the forces that defeated Nazism, the extreme degenerative form of the crisis of the national state, and have sustained the world political system that has guaranteed international order and economic development in the second post-war period. This theory of international relations has allowed it to give a fundamental contribution to understanding the influence that the international political system exerts on economic development and in particular on the economy's tendency to internationalization.

Lionel Robbins' (1898–1984) thinking is normally associated with the liberal theory and is rightly criticized for its opposition to the growing state-intervention in the economy, which is necessary for dealing with problems like employment or regional unbalance. But his contribution to the analysis of the political conditions necessary to let the market and economic planning function at international level is usually forgotten. In *Economic Planning and International Order* (1937) he observed that the market is an institution needing "an apparatus for maintaining law and order. But whereas *within* national areas such apparatus, however imperfect, existed, *between* national areas there was no apparatus at all." Not to have taken into account that difference has been a serious mistake by most of the liberals of the 19th century.

> Within the national areas they relied upon the coercive power of the state to provide the restraints which harmonized the interests of the different individuals. Between the areas they relied only upon demonstration of common interest and the futility of violence: their outlook here, that is to say, was implicitly not liberal, but anarchist (Robbins L., 1937, 241).

In fact, market laws cannot function without a coercive power giving everybody a legal guarantee, and juridical and administrative regulations channeling economic activity within the banks of law. But in a world of sovereign states the political worries of a defensive and offensive character tend to prevail over those of a strictly economic character regarding the most productive use of resources. Thus, productive resources are organized taking into account more the state's security requirements that the welfare of the citizens. In such a context, one may understand protectionism and economic nationalism, which spread in the whole industrialized world in the period of the world wars. Once the historical phase of Great Britain's naval and trading hegemony, that had guaranteed the unity of the world market, finished, international anarchy got worse and the need of economic self-sufficiency, vital for ensuring the State's independence in case of war, became ever more worrying. National states placed their trust in protectionism to get economic self-sufficiency. So, unlike the explanations of Marxist inspiration, which ascribe protectionism to the monopolistic structure of the economic system, for Robbins its ultimate cause is international anarchy.

He argued on this matter in *The Economic Causes of War* (1939), where he disproved the two main theories on imperialism of Marxist inspiration: that by Rosa Luxemburg (1870–1919) and that by Lenin. He notes that in defining the historical context giving birth to conflicts among states in the contemporary world, when the tendency to internationalize the production process is dominant, one cannot but take into account the economic damage suffered by every state caused by its being excluded from trading with the territories subject to the sovereignty of other states. This means that the governments' behaviour is influenced a great deal by the necessity to extend as much as possible the area in which that damage does not exist and to exclude from this area the other governments. If, for example, raw materials are situated in territories that may become not-accessible in case of war, it will be in the interest of every state to try and extend its sovereignty over these territories, because the availability of raw materials is the condition for economic, political and military independence.

In conditions of peace, accessibility to raw materials is just a matter of price. But since the world situation is dominated by war or the threat of war, the struggle for the control of raw materials, from which no state wants to be excluded, becomes a reason of conflict among states. The rush to the partition of colonies at the end of the 1800s illustrates very well how this mechanism was operating. But the political context that makes it possible is the organization of the world in sovereign states; instead, a reorganization of international relations, and in particular of those among the European states, in a federal sense would subject it to a rational and democratic control, eliminating the factor that turns economic conflicts into military conflicts.

The fact is that "there is world economy. But there is no world polity" (Robbins, 1937, 239). The control of the economy, be it of a liberal or a socialist kind, is possible only on a national level, hence it is inefficient. Thus, "international liberalism is not a plan which has been tried and failed. It is a plan which has never been carried through—a revolution crushed by reaction before it had time to be fully tested" (*ibid.*, 238). The same conclusions can be extended to the socialist plan.

Going a little beyond Robbins' conclusions and reminding Kant's model of a future society, one can say that the full realization of liberty and equality can only be possible in the framework of a world federation, which eliminates force relations among states and guarantees peace. Robbins' standpoint, if properly applied to other cases, allows him to highlight the limits not only of liberalism, but also of democracy and socialism, since they are not in control of all the conditions for their realization. In fact, the struggle for liberty and equality has taken place separately, nation by nation, while mankind's division in rival states has made the results of those struggles partial and precarious. The crisis of these ideologies, ever more evident and by now widely recognized in contemporary history, has its root in the national limit of their vision and of their field of action. That limit has given rise to a wrong idea of peace, seen as the automatic consequence of the establishment of liberalism, democracy or socialism in every state. Instead, peace requires an *ad-hoc* struggle whose aim is to defeat and control the authoritarian and belligerent tendencies, dominant in a world of sovereign states. In this sense peace appears to be the condition for fully developing the values of liberty and equality.

This profound political thinking was not without influence on political reality. It influenced Winston Churchill, who on 16 June 1940, for strengthening the resistance to Nazism, proposed to France, which was about to fall under German rule, to join Great Britain, instituting a Parliament, a government, and an army in common (Churchill W. S., 1949, 180–184, vol. 2). When Churchill wrote in his memoirs of the War Cabinet's discussion about the proposal that "France and Britain shall no longer be two nations, but one Franco-British Union," he expressed his surprise when he saw "the staid, solid, experienced politicians engage themselves so passionately in an immense design" (Churchill W. S., 1949, 180–184, vol. 2). It is to be noted that three members of Churchill's Cabinet were supporters of Federal Union: Clement Attlee (1927–1991), the Lord Privy Seal, Ernest Bevin (1881–1951), Minister of Labour and Sir Archibald Sinclair (1890–1970), Air Minister. Charles Kimber (born in 1912), one of the three founders of Federal Union who witnessed to those events, wrote that the action of Federal Union was so penetrating that it can "claim, with some justification to have brought the offer of union with France within the 'art of the possible' (at least in that desperate moment). But it also can claim to have put federation at the top of the agenda of such public discussion of 'war aims'" (Kimber C., 2005, 13).

The author of Churchill's plan was Jean Monnet (1888–1979), who devoted the first chapter of his *Memoirs* to the narration of this event. When

France was occupied by the Nazi army, he was at London, where he was President of Franco-British co-ordination committee, created to organize a joint military action. Monnet's special talent lay in his capacity to influence crucial decisions, working far from the limelight, in the background where the future is prepared patiently. After the war he became a protagonist of European unification.

In the moment of the collapse of the European system, for the first time a national government, reversing the system's historical tendency to work on the principle of the balance of power among independent states, was formulating a proposal of federal unification. The significance of that proposal is clear: the federal principle had become an operational political objective. Unfortunately, that proposal did not find in the defeated French government an interlocutor ready to accept such a revolutionary project, and it was dropped. Thus, Europe did not enter a road that could have led it to its federal unification around a first Anglo-French core.

There is to mention that on December 18, 1941, right after the Pearl Harbour attack, on the *New York Times* an appeal was published in favour of a federation of democracies, seen as a first step towards the world federation, inspired by Clarence Streit's ideas and signed by renowned persons, like Harold Ickes (1874–1952), Secretary of State for Internal Affairs, Owen Roberts (1875–1955), Supreme Court judge, John Foster Dulles (1888–1959), who will become Secretary of State in Eisenhower's (1890–1969) administration, and Grenville Clark (1882–1967), one of the founders of the World Federalist Movement. The initiative, which had the unofficial support of the US government, has a similar meaning to that promoted by Churchill the year before. Like the latter, it had no effect. However, from it the ideas arose that gave birth to the Atlantic Alliance.

The Federal Union movement, which in the period between the two world wars had contributed to shedding light on the sense of the choice Europe was faced with (the alternative between unity in an imperial form, brought about by violence, and unity among democratic states, founded on consent), after the second World War faded out. And this happened just when the historical conditions had ripened for starting Europe's unification process. This paradoxical fact highlights the limits of a purely technical conception of federalism (meant as the theory of the federal State) peculiar of the culture of the Federal Union's leading group.

This is the limit of the ideas presented by Kenneth C. Wheare (1907–1979) in his excellent comparative analysis on federal government, which is defined "that method of dividing powers so that that the general and regional governments are each, within a sphere, co-ordinate and independent" (Wheare K.C., 1966, 11). This formula allows us to clearly distinguish the federation from its two contiguous, but qualitatively different, types of political organization: the confederation and the unitary state with a regional decentralization system. A confederation is not a state, but a form of international organization in which the institutions of the Union are subordinated to the member states. Regional decentralization is one of the possible institutional arrangements of the unitary state, in which the regions are subordinated to the central government.

For these authors, federalism has never been presented as an autonomous ideology with its own standpoint over history, society, power, values and other ideologies. The Anglo-Saxon federalists never went so far as to work out, as the Italian ones did after *The Ventotene Manifesto*—we will see it later—, a conception of federalism as the basis of a new political behaviour able to take it into action and to let it live on as an organization disengaged from political parties, as the Italian federalists did after the failure of the first attempt to establish a European federation when the European Defence Community and the European Political Community fell. The choice of federalism as a criterion of political action would have allowed to consolidate the priority of the European federation and peace over any other political or social objective, and in particular over the priority given to national objectives that guides the behaviour of political parties.

For Robbins, as for all the other liberal notables that joined Federal Union, federalism never became a priority political choice, but remained an idea ancillary to liberalism. The same is true for Barbara Wootton and socialism. In essence, the federal institutions and peace were simply considered as means for making the full realization of liberalism or socialism possible. The choice to constitute a federalist movement in Great Britain was determined by the dramatic contingency of the second World War, but, in the changed historical context of the post-war times, many of British federalists abandoned the prospective of a European federation.

Robbins's political journey represents one individual aspect of a wider collective phenomenon: the rise and decline of Federal Union.

The final chapter of *The Economic Causes of War* was a passionate peroration for the United States of Europe. Here he clarified his position on the relationship between world, Atlantic and European federalism. The third objective represented, at that time, his first priority. He qualified "utopian" a federation of world dimensions, since "there is not sufficient feeling of a common citizenship," there is "no sufficiently generalized culture" and "even the electoral problems of such a body would present insurmountable difficulties" (Robbins L., 1939, 105). We could add another outstanding difficulty, which was still present after the World Wars, especially during the Cold War, namely the deep cleavages which were dividing the states in the international system. Of course, a world federation is "the divine event towards which all that is good in the heritage of the diverse civilizations of the world, invites us to strive"(Robbins L., 1939, 105). But it is a distant ultimate goal of human history.

As regards the Atlantic federation, it is to note that Robbins had expressed his scepticism at Streit's project for a federal union of democracies, including the United States. In his opinion, the US, unlike the European states, did not have a strong interest to build a federal union with other states. He considered "very unlikely that [. . .] the citizens of the United States will feel that compelling urge to union with other peoples" (Robbins L., 1939, 106).

On the contrary, in Robbins's opinion, it is not utopian to strive for a federation in Europe, where the economic and technological evolution was imposing the overcoming of national sovereignties.

> As gunpowder rendered obsolete the feudal system—Robbins wrote—so the aeroplane renders obsolete the system of the independent sovereignties of Europe. [He concluded with this cogent argumentation]: a more comprehensive type of organization is inevitable. Will it come by mutual agreement or by caesarian conquest? That is the unsolved question. For either there must be empire or federation; on a long view, there is no alternative (Robbins L., 1939, 107).

Unlike Lord Lothian, the other towering exponent of British federalism, who died in 1940 during World War Two, Robbins lived until 1984. Thus, he witnessed the development of European unification until the direct election of the European Parliament. He never repudiated either the idea of the decline of the nation-states or his attachment for the concept of federalism. But what is paradoxical is the fact that Robbins, who had been one of the most brilliant advocates of European federalism gave up this specific cause by just at the moment, after the war, when the political conditions for European unification were ripening. In his autobiography he wrote that:

> When the United Europe movement was first launched in the shape of proposals for the Coal and Steel Community, I opposed it. I opposed it, not because I had in any way abandoned my desire for the creation of larger units, but rather because I thought that the creation of this larger unit ran the danger of being inimical to the creation of a still larger one, or at any rate to forms of political and economic co-operation over a wide area which were essential if the Western world were not to fall apart (Robbins L., 1971, 238).

The larger unit to which Robbins was referring to was the Atlantic Community. Robbins wrote that during the war he

> became more and more convinced of the indispensability of continued American co-operation in maintaining the balance of the world. In two world wars the

nations of Europe had not succeeded in solving their problems unaided. [Consequently], a continuation, in some form or other, of political and military association between ourselves and the two great unions of North America seemed to me to be the *sine qua non* for any hope of preserving the civilization of the West (Robbins L., 1971, 236).

One reason for his disenchantment with the European federalist cause was the anti-Americanism characterizing the attitudes of many intellectuals and politicians especially in France. It was only in 1960, during a speech delivered in Rome (Robbins L., 1961, 154–155), that Robbins admitted his mistake. The extraordinary success of the European Community obliged him to change his mind.

This state of uncertainty with regard to the European federation shows that Robbins, despite he gave a federalist interpretation of some aspects of the contemporary world, had kept a traditional vision of history, seen as the struggle between the principles of liberty and authoritarianism, which in the second post-war period took a visible form in the rivalry between the United States and the Soviet Union, and was perceived as a planetary clash between democracy and communism. He failed to realize that a successful development of federalism through European unification was in fact essential for the prevalence of pluralist democracy in Europe, rather than authoritarian Soviet communism, as the framework for the development of liberalism, as he would have wished, or of other legitimate manifestations of democratic politics. Nor did he realize that the cohesion of the Atlantic Alliance was dependent on the hegemony of the US and that the European federation would have laid the foundations for an equal partnership between Europe and America. Moreover, in his view, the European unification was not felt as the start of the process of mankind's unification, which, although starting in one continent, affects the whole world and whose ultimate goal is the building of peace, but as an element of the struggle for the defence and the expansion of Western values against the communist world. This attitude leads to a national policy which in practice places the strengthening of the established powers, in particular the bipolar arrangement of world power, before the building of new regional-dimension powers in the perspective of forming a multipolar world system and a further overcoming of it in the world federation.

The difficulty for federalism in Great Britain to continue as an independent theory and organization is also due to the fact that here the crisis of the national state occurred in a milder form: the defeat of nationalism in the second World War was not as full of consequences as it was on the continent. And this explains Great Britain's delay in entering the European Community. Immediately after the war, having won the war and not having suffered, unlike France, the humiliation of a Nazi invasion, it kept the Empire and with it the illusion to be the third world power. When it lost the Empire, it developed the project to manage its political decline with a bigger margin of international autonomy than the other Western European countries, trying to play the role of the United States' privileged ally in the shadow of the American hegemony. Only in 1961, five years after the failure of the Suez expedition, which inflicted a serious blow to Great Britain's role in the world, did it come to the decision to join the European Community, that materialized in 1973.

Chapter Seven

The Rise of the Theoretical Autonomy of Federalism after the Second World War

7.1 RISE AND CRISIS OF THE INSTITUTIONAL APPROACH

In the era of the world wars and especially after the second World War, federalism has broadened its coverage in order to adjust to the changes that have taken place in the contemporary world.

One direction in which the federalist theory has developed is the one called *new federalism*. This field of studies aims to adjust the federalist model to the changes that have taken place in contemporary societies. The first change is its trend towards centralization, which is the consequence of the pressures exerted by two factors. Firstly, the industrial revolution has made ever more frequent the production and exchange relations across the borders of the member states, transforming a group of mostly agricultural communities, relatively isolated from each other, into a unified economic and social system. The federated states have lost control of these processes to the benefit of the federal governments that have taken the lead in governing the economy and in building the welfare state. The second centralizing factor has its roots in the pressure exerted on federal governments by the world system of states, which does not allow any state to decide to isolate itself. In fact, the world wars and the persistence of strong international tensions in the second post-war period have forced them to create huge bureaucratic and military apparatuses at the service of the security and power needs of federal governments.

According to some authors, the trend to concentrate power in federal governments would be balanced by a centrifugal thrust coming from the giant corporations. According to Adolf A. Berle Jr. (1895–1971), a new form of "economic federalism" would have developed (Berle A. A. Jr., 73), characterized by the emergence of strong economic-power concentrations that are

replacing political pluralism, which is declining because of the loss of autonomy by the federated states. To this theory one can object that the economic-in-
terest groups cannot create constitutional balances, but they only adjust themselves to existing balances. They exert a pressure on governments and
Parliaments so as to get decisions in their favour. And if power is concentrated,
their interest would be addressed most of all to the central power. The growth
of giant corporations does not constitute, therefore, an alternative to centralization in federal states, but it is, instead, a factor reinforcing that trend. That theory is masking the true nature of changes, like the trend to centralization, that
have deeply altered the nature of federal institutions in the contemporary world.

The second trend is the rise of co-operative federalism. Originally the federal state, in conformity with the conditions of mostly-agricultural societies,
was characterized by scant relations among the states governments and between these and the federal government. But with the growth of industrialization, in order to prevent the increased intervention-capability of public
powers (and in federal states this trend has also affected the regional governments) from generating conflicts, quite dangerous for the federal balance, a
co-operative model between the federal government and the states governments has asserted itself everywhere. Whereas in the classical or dual model
of federalism competences were divided between the two government levels
according to the criterion of exclusivity, spelled out in the Tenth Amendment
of the US Constitution—which grants to the states all the powers not explicitly granted to the federal government—, in the model of co-operative federalism all the competences tend to become shared.

From these considerations the need emerges to give a definition of federal
institutions that includes the notions of dual federalism and co-operative federalism. To this end, here is the definition given by Maurice J. Vile (born in
1927):

> Federalism is a system of government in which the central and the regional au-
> thorities are linked in a mutually interdependent political relationship; in this
> system a balance is maintained such as no one of the government levels be-
> comes dominant to the point of being able to impose decisions to the other, but
> each can influence, negotiate with and persuade the other (Vile M. J., 199).

Another development line of the federalist theory is represented by the
trend to overcome the institutional approach, which reduces federalism to a
mere constitutional technique. It originates from some of the most significant
transformations under way today, that are assuming federal features: the
spread of the federal model in large states of the Third World, like Nigeria and
India, the crisis of the unitary national state, the tendency to form multi-

national political unities and to unify great regions of the world, and the tendency to regional and local self-government.

In its attempt to interpreting these new processes, the federalist thought has enriched itself with new categories for analysis, progressively asserting its theoretical autonomy up to the point of adopting an autonomous standpoint of its own over history, society, politics and values, that is to say, up to presenting itself as a new ideology. In such a perspective, I will take under consideration four models: federalism as a process, integral federalism, federalism as an ideology, and world federalism.

The model worked out by Carl J. Friedrich (1901–1984) in *Trends of Federalism in Theory and Practice*, which describes *federalism as a process*, highlights some limits of the institutional approach. He contrasts the institutional definition of classical federalism, which was interested in particular in problems of sovereignty, distribution of powers and the structure of the institutions, with his dynamic approach. Friedrich constructs federalist theory privileging political and social change and the historical development of federal relationships at the expense of the structural and institutional aspects. Every particular variety of federal organization represents a stage in the development of a political and social reality in continuous evolution. What distinguishes federalism, according to Friedrich, is the requirement of maintaining unity in diversity in a process of continuous reciprocal adaptation of the common organization and the component parts. This balance between conflicting tendencies avoids the opposing dangers of centralization (which would transform the federal system into a unitary state) and separatism (which would split up the federation).

He defines the federation as "a union of groups, united by one or more common objectives, rooted in common values, interests or beliefs, but retaining their distinctive group character for other purposes" (Friedrich C.J., 177). This is a definition which may be applied to a great variety of political organizations: a federal state, a confederation of states, an alliance of states, a unitary state with regional and local self-government, an association of non-governmental organizations, such as political parties, trade-unions, political movements, interest groups, churches and so forth.

In Friedrich's opinion, federalism is the result of two different processes: integration or differentiation. In the first, two or more political communities join for solving together common problems, each keeping its independence. In the second, a political community with a unitary structure undergoes a differentiation process, giving rise to a set of independent political entities, which do not question, however, the unity of the overall political framework.

The life of every federation is the result of a permanent tension between the unitary tendency and the pluralistic tendency. Both in the process of integration and the process of differentiation, the basic objective of federalism is to limit centralized power, by dividing it up. In the first case, the birth of a federal government limits the powers of the states who participate in the federative process, in the second case, the formation of independent political communities within a unitary state limits the power of central government.

Friedrich's objective is to base the notion of federalism on the overcoming of the traditional unitary sovereign state. His dynamic approach allows him to emphasize the federative processes tending to overcome the unitary state upwards and downwards, through the creation of autonomous communities above and within that polity.

When he insists on the two directions of the federative process, he is suggesting new categories that let us appreciate some tendencies presently under way: that to overcoming the unitary state and forming states or international organizations of continental or sub-continental dimensions; and that to decentralizing power and to achieving regional and local self-government within the old unitary states. Friedrich's basic thesis seems to confirm the inadequacy of the mere institutional approach in the study of federalism. In fact, it is not possible to understand federal institutions without understanding the historical and social processes that set in motion the institutional mechanisms.

Once we have clarified the limits to a purely institutional approach, it is still necessary to reflect on the relationships existing between institutions and the historical process. In general terms institutions are a product of the historical process (for example, representative democracy within national states in unthinkable outside the framework of the industrial revolution). Moreover, institutions are an indispensable condition for the existence of the historical process itself. Using figurative language, we may say they are like the banks of a river within which the historical and social processes flow. Were it not contained within these banks, the drift of the current would be lost and history would have no sense, in the double acceptation of this word: direction and meaning. The institutions are thus instruments by means of which men try to control history. This means that institutions have "*relative independence*" with regard to the historical process, that is they tend to channel the new processes along old riverbeds, but "*ultimately*" they are forced to bend to the stream of history. In other words, when the institutions are no longer suited to containing new processes, the latter burst their banks and create new ones, that fall in line with the changes of history.

Above I used a few expressions in italics and inverted commas which can be read in some letters written late in his life by Friedrich Engels, which have an important methodological content. He stated that "According to the materialist conception of history, the *ultimately* determining element in history is the production and reproduction of real life" (Engels F., September 21, 1890). On the other hand, "the state [. . .] the new independent power, while having in the main to follow the movement of production, also, owing to its inward independence (the *relative independence* originally transferred to it and gradually further developed) reacts in its turn upon the conditions and course of production" (Engels F., October 27, 1890).

This means that, while the rather insignificant changes in the mode of production do not have any repercussion on political institutions, the important changes in the mode of production upset political structures and force them to fall into line with the mode of production. The relationship between the productive structure and the political superstructure is, according to Engels's formula, "an interaction of two unequal forces." The reaction of the state can run in the same direction of the evolution of the productive process, then "development is more rapid," or it can oppose the line of development, in which case "state power [. . .] will go to pieces in the long run" (Engels F., October 27, 1890).

However, by exclusively stressing the historical and social processes, Friedrich neglects the role of institutions in history. He stated that "no sovereignty can exist in a federal system; autonomy and sovereignty exclude each other in such a political order. To speak of the transfer of a part of the sovereignty is to deny the idea of sovereignty which since Bodin has meant indivisibility. No one has 'the last word'. The idea of a compact is inherent in federalism, and the 'constituent power', which makes the compact, takes the place of the sovereign" (Friedrich C.J., 8). In the dynamic model proposed by Friedrich, the confederation is conceived as a stage in the federative process. He sets no value on the difference between federation and confederation, which is defined "the quintessence of the static and formalistic approach" (Friedrich C.J., 82). A confederation is conceived as a stage in the federative process, and in comparison with the federation it is not considered as something qualitatively different, but just as a weaker form of political organization (Friedrich C.J., 11–12). A wrong conclusion of this theory is that he considers the result of the British Empire's transformation process into the Commonwealth as an example of federation (Friedrich C.J., 83).

Actually, the institutional viewpoint still plays an irreplaceable role as a criterion for evaluating the nature and trends of federative processes. Understanding the structure of a federation is necessary for helping us ascertain when a federative process has produced a federation, for finding out whether the process has federative features and, if the answer is positive, for measuring the progress achieved in building a federation. The institutional notion of federation lets us state, for example, that the Commonwealth is not a federation, and that there are no appreciable signs that it is going to be one. On the other hand, a confederation is not always a stage in a process leading to a federation. History shows countless examples of confederations that dissolved before reaching the goal of a federation.

There can be no doubt, moreover, that federal organization is incompatible with the traditional concept of sovereignty. At the same time, it is worth recalling that the requirement of an authority which ultimately imposes its decision on the entire territory of the state is a basic achievement for the modern state. The novelty of federal institutions consists in the fact that the distribution of power is organized in such a way that certain centres of power have the last word on certain matters, others on others, without hierarchical relationships between the various sovereign powers. We should also remember that generally in federations there is an authority with ultimate powers of decision, in the case of conflict between the independent governments among whom power is divided. The courts have the power to annul laws which do not comply with the Constitution and to order all powers to comply with the Constitution.

All the works of Daniel J. Elazar (1934–1999) are devoted to the aim to formulate federalism in such a way as to widen its reach in time and space. His field of research, that initially was limited to the study of the US federal system, thought of as a new principle of power organization within a single polity, was progressively enlarged in two directions: firstly, in a historical and comparative perspective, with the aim to analyse and classify all the examples of federal organizations (Elazar D.J., 1991); and then in an ever wider international context, with the aim to extend the federal principle to the entire planet (Elazar D.J., 1998).

First of all, Elazar says that the first formulation of a federalist idea has a theological origin. It dates back to the Jewish idea of covenant found in the Bible. The Jewish word *brit*, like the Latin *foedus* (from which the word federalism is derived), means pact. This concept was used to define the covenant between God and man, and between God and the people of Israel. What the religious idea of covenant has more than the political ones of treaty and constitutional pact, is the depth of the commitment that binds the parties, and the belief of its being in accordance with the Creator's will. Moreover, according to Elazar, the principles of federalism were already applied in the political realm by the ancient Jews since the 13th century B.C., when the tribes of Israel united in a covenant of a federal type. Finally, the application of the federal paradigm to politics is connected with a vision of the history of mankind whose target is the Messianic era, when a universal union of all nations will be realized, each keeping its own identity. According to Elazar, in the course of history other peoples experimented federal-type institutions, for example the leagues of cities in ancient Greece, in medieval Italy and Germany, the Holy Roman Empire, the Swiss Confederation, the United Provinces of the Netherlands.

The Biblical idea of covenant was proposed again in the 16th and 17th centuries in the form of a "federal theology" by the movements of the Protestant Reformation, especially the Huguenots, the Calvinists and the English and American Puritans, and it eventually resulted in political ideas, formulated in particular by Johannes Althusius (1557–1638), which contributed to defining several aspects of politics and the state in the modern and contemporary world: contractualism, seen no longer as a unilateral political obligation by the people towards the Prince, but as a mutual obligation between two parties; the right to resist against tyranny and monarchical absolutism; local self-government; the social pluralism of intermediate bodies and the political pluralism of local bodies.

Elazar recognizes that the birth of the United States marks a turn in the history of federalism, which from that moment on assumes the modern features it has kept to this day. In *The Federalist* there is the definition of a form of power sharing between the federal government and the states' governments which has become the model for the other federal systems.

The decline of the national state, the form of political organization that assembles all powers in one center, has opened new prospects to federalism, through the ensuing reorganization of institutions and the transfer of power upwards (the international organizations) and downwards (the smaller territorial communities). All new federal governmental arrangements "embody the idea of a more than one government exercising powers over the same territory. That idea,—Elazar noted—which was at the heart of the American invention of federalism, was anathema to the European fathers of the modern nation—state" (Elazar J. D., 1987, 225). It is an idea that answers to a widespread need in contemporary society. On the one hand, forming polities of larger dimensions than traditional nations allows them to profit by their large size on the economic and strategic plane. On the other, developing regional and local self-government forms allows them to organize social differences, often of an ethnic nature, within the old national states, to promote the formation of cross-border regions covering territories of two or more national states and to compound the formation of larger polities with the diversity and autonomy of smaller territorial communities.

Elazar, in tune with Friedrich's thesis, felt the need to simultaneously study federal institutions and federative processes. Thus, he worked out a list of the types of institutional arrangements that originate from the erosion process of the national state's centralized structure in two directions: upwards (confederations, like the European Union; federacies, like the agreement between the United States and Puerto Rico; customs unions, like the European Economic Community; leagues of states based on common cultural links, like the Arab League; condominiums, like Andorra; etc.) and downwards (regional autonomies, like the ordinary regions in Italy; cultural self-governments, like in

Belgium; regional autonomies based on an international treaty, like the Alto
Adige region in Italy; provinces or national districts, like in the Russian Federation; etc.). Almost none of these institutions has a federal character in a
strict sense. However, they are the expression of the crisis of the national state
as a self-sufficient political formula and of the need to overcome its closed
and centralized structure. Elazar remarks that almost all of the existing states
(starting with those of the European continent) are involved in processes
tending to limit their sovereignty. This is the general direction taken by political changes and by the course of history.

Elazar studies federalism as a method of political integration (1984). It
stands out as an alternative to the centralization model: a network of power
centres whose cohesion is not measured by the force of the centre versus the
periphery, but rather by the force of its overall structure, consisting in a system of interdependent power centres. Therefore, federalism appears to be a
very efficient institutional device for political integration, for ensuring the
functioning of pluralistic societies, for protecting minorities, for solving ethnic, religious and national conflicts, and for answering to the need of peace
and international solidarity. The European Union is the world region that has
progressed the most along this road. Its present structure has a confederal
character, even if it is "a new type of confederation" (Elazar J. D., 1999, 484),
which progressively transfers functions to the European level in sectors
where the states have agreed to do that for pursuing common objectives.
Elazar does not limit himself to analyzing and classifying the federal systems,
but considers federalism as "a great [political] design," suitable for governing
the social transformations under way in the contemporary world. In particular, the building of European unity has reached such a degree of maturity that
by now the problem is to bring it to conclusion and make it irreversible by
drafting a Constitution (Elazar J. D., 1999, 487).

Like other federalist authors who lived in the 20th century (for example,
Marc and Albertini), Elazar pushes his research in the direction of global-
ity. His last book (1998) is devoted to globalization and to the potential the
federalist design has to extend itself beyond national borders up to embrace the whole planet and to "constitutionalize globalization." This
means, in other terms, to govern the globalization process by building a
world order that has the federalist constitutionalism as its cornerstone, but
it is convenient here to specify that by that expression Elazar means a confederal order.

According to Elazar, the state-centric paradigm is superseded by a new paradigm, that some way or other affects all of the states of this planet and which
nobody can escape. It is the tendency to establish everywhere agreements or
systems of a confederal character.

These confederal solutions, [. . .] ranging from full-fledged confederations to little more than very limited-purpose associations of states. [. . .] They vary in the degree to which they constitutionally or empirically bind their members. In fact, they are all of limited purpose and collectively consist of a myriad of overlapping relationships. Even more critically is that the strongest of them have become what we may call constitutionally binding (Elazar J. D., 1998, 6).

The expansion of the web of confederal arrangements at international level is associated with the dismantling of the centralized structures of the nation-states and the increase of the autonomy of the regional and local communities, which entails a change of paradigm in the study of politics. Elazar said:

It is too early to predict whether these confederations and confederal arrangements will succeed as such, but the changes are that the development of world-wide, multilateral, overlapping, linking institutions embracing formally sovereign states, to which all nations will have to be attached in one way or another, offers the opportunity for and will place demands on smaller nationalisms and localisms to find their place in the sun through confederal political arrangements of one sort or another. These may still be called 'statehood' and 'sovereignty', but with a very different meaning than those terms had during the modern epoch. The modern terms may survive, but implicit within them will be federal limitations of one kind or another, somewhere between the constituent states of federations and the sovereign states defined and recognized by modern international law. Even international law is beginning to reflect this paradigm change. Modern international law was born in the years following the Treaty of Westphalia to embody the new state system. [. . .] In time it became one of the greatest barriers to the introduction of a federalist paradigm because practitioners in the international arena were trained [. . .] to think and talk in term of state sovereignty (Elazar J. D., 1998, 147–148).

Elazar cannot be accused of not being able to understand the difference between a federation and a confederation. He said that "federalism [. . .] in its modern form is a variation of the federal system invented in the United States [. . .] and embodied in the American federal Constitution, written in 1787" (Elazar J. D., 1987, 38–39), of which he acknowledges the institutional innovation and the discontinuity with the previous forms of political organization, which had a confederal character. The definition he gives of federalism is quite comprehensive:

The essence of federalism is not to be found in a particular set of institutions, but in institutionalization of particular relationships among the participants in political life. Consequently, federalism is a phenomenon that provides many options for the organization of political authority and power; as long as the proper

relations are created, a wide variety of political structures can be developed that
are consistent with the federal principles. (Elazar J. D., 1987, 12).

A federal organization is instituted and regulated by a covenant—"the term
federal means covenant," argued Elazar.

Federal principles are concerned with the combination of self-rule and shared
rule As a political principle, federalism has to do with the constitutional diffusion of power so that the constituting elements in a federal arrangement share in
the process of common policy making and administration by right, while the activities of the common government are conducted in such a way as to maintain
their respective integrities (Elazar J. D., 1987, 5–6).

It is a system of government that can hold only if it rests on a maximum of
consensus and if it resorts to a minimum of coercion. In addition, Elazar
maintained that there is an inseparable link between modern federalism and
the republican and democratic form of government. "Federalism—he
wrote—by its very nature must be republican. The American federal system
was the first modern federal polity clearly to link federalism and popular government, or democracy" (Elazar J. D., 1987, 107–108). There is to remind
here that this principle was enunciated by Kant in the first definitive article of
Perpetual Peace, and is contained in the Constitution of the United States,
which provides that the federal government shall assure to the member states
the republican form of government. This requirement allows us to distinguish
a federation from other forms of political organization in which several independent and coordinated power centres are present, like the ancient state of
Israel or the Holy Roman Empire; despite that, they were constituted before
representative democracy was established.

Considering federalism a genus so broad as to include among its species
the confederal institutions, the leagues of states, the administratively decentralized states or even the colonial regimes, Elazar falls into the trap that had
led Friedrich off the right track. While it is true that the above mentioned institutional arrangements may be the expression of federative processes, it is
also true that they may not be so, as shown by many examples of confederations of states and decentralized unitary states that did not turn into federations. The only way to ascertain which direction a supposed federative
process is going is to keep in mind the distinction between a federation and
its two contiguous, but qualitatively different, types of political organization:
the confederation and the unitary state with regional decentralization. The
confederation is an international organization subordinate to its member
states, which remain, therefore, fully sovereign. The regional decentralization

is one of the possible arrangements of a unitary state, to which the regions and the other local bodies remain subordinate. Only the federation is a form of state that institutes an independent power centre (the federal government) which coexists with other independent powers (the federated communities). Thus, it is advisable to reserve the attribute of "federal" to the institutions possessing such requisites.

The study of the institutional evolution of international organizations and of the states with regional autonomies can provide some elements for judging whether a federative process is under way or not. Let us consider, for example, the structure and the institutional evolution of the European Community and Union. The European Community, since its inception, has been showing its contradictory character, which derives from the intertwining of international with governmental elements or more precisely of federal and confederal elements. Even though in the EU there are institutions which have a federal character, they co-exist with some intergovernmental institutions peculiar to an intergovernmental organization. However, the evolution of the EU reveals a tendency to reinforcing and democratizing its institutions. The European Court of Justice has asserted with its rulings the primacy of the European law over the national. The European Parliament after its election by universal suffrage has increased its co-decision powers with the Council, and by instituting the euro and the European Central Bank the decision has been taken to transfer monetary sovereignty to the European level. Considering all this, one can state that an institutional evolution is under way, tending towards a federal outcome, even if, admittedly, that is not certain, and standstills and even regressions can occur.

Instead, it is reasonable to express the opposite judgment about the prospects of the Commonwealth, which, after the Statute of Westminster (1931) and even more so after the second World War, has shown a clear tendency towards its break up, and a willingness by its member states to join various regional organizations. The United Kingdom has adhered to the European Community in 1973, and this choice signals its definitive renunciation to the project of being a party in world politics at the head of the Commonwealth. The Constitutions of Canada and Australia, which were incorporated in laws of the Westminster Parliament, have been "repatriated," and thus most of the remaining limitations to the full assertion of the sovereignty of those countries have been removed. This emancipation from the dependence on London brought with it the choice to join various regional organizations: Canada has joined the NAFTA and the APEC, Australia has joined the ASEAN, the APEC and the South Pacific Forum. A similar trend was shown by the Commonwealth members located in Asia, Africa, the Caribbean and the Pacific.

A second objection concerns the question whether it is appropriate to call "Constitution," as Elazar does, the document that defines the structure of a confederation. Actually, the distinction between federation and confederation defines by itself the boundary between what is to be placed on a constitutional plane, hence belongs to the sphere of statehood, and what is to be placed on the plane of international relations, hence belongs to the sphere of force relations among states. A confederation is not a constitutional order, but an international organization. Therefore, the document defining its structure and functions, in Wheare's opinion, "should be called more appropriately agreement, pact, or treaty" (Wheare K.C., 1966, 24).

A third objection concerns the federation's democratic structure. If it is true, as Elazar says, that representative democracy is a feature that characterizes the federal institutions, one has to make the history of federalism start with the US Constitution. There ensues that all previous political formations must be excluded from the category of federalism, because, although they were provided with a territorial power sharing, they did not have a democratic regime. This means that the ancient state of Israel or the Holy Roman Empire may be considered at the most as formations forerunning federalism, lacking one of its essential requirements.

7.2 INTEGRAL FEDERALISM

In the dark years of nationalism's undisputed sway, around the review *L'Ordre Nouveau*, published in Paris from 1933 to 1938, a federalist group was formed that continued to be active also after the second World War principally in France; its most notable members were Robert Aron (1898–1975), Arnaud Dandieu (1891–1933), Alexandre Marc (1904–2000) and Denis de Rougemont (1891–1985). They worked out a doctrine that advocated a brand-new model of society and State, founded on an "integral," i.e. not only institutional, but also social, economic and philosophical, idea of federalism.

Integral federalism is an overall response to the problems of our times and is based on a comprehensive judgment of the contemporary world: the global crisis of our civilization. This means that all the institutions which govern our society are obsolete and no longer fit to a reality in rapid transformation. Contemporary man is dominated and oppressed by big mass organizations (giant corporations, political parties, trade unions, bureaucratic machineries, nation-states) that characterize mass society, in which social relations are depersonalised. The breakdown of social-solidarity relations, arising from the violent clashes between the big mass-organizations, is matched by the anarchy created by state sovereignties at the international level, and both of them cause an abnormal growth of the centralized power of the state and of its bureaucratic and military apparatuses. At the root of this crisis there is an individualistic culture, originating from Jacobinism. It has determined the atomization of society, the dissolution of all the "intermediate bodies" and has laid the foundations for the fascist and communist totalitarianisms of our era.

In the wake of Tocqeville's and Proudhon's analysis, integral federalism is critical of the centralizing character of the state born out of the French Revolution, which, leaving no room to any organization mediating between the individual and the state, becomes potentially totalitarian. Democratic centralism permits people's participation in the making of political decisions only at the level of national Parliament, and the regime of political parties demands to give the monopoly of the representation of public opinion to the professionals of politics, who control closed, oligarchical and bureaucratic organizations.

The federalist alternative wants to overturn this reality. Aron and Marc define federalism as

> the political idea which allows individual liberties to be compounded with the need to organize the collectivity [and which] makes easier the existence of free human communities, able [. . .] to associate themselves without losing, by doing that, their peculiar characters" (Aron R., Marc A., 1948, 19).

In other terms, federalism is a form of political organization that makes a combination of liberty and authority, unity and diversity, possible. If federalism is defined in such vague terms, it is possible to find traces of it in every epoch, even "since those uncertain origins of history when human communities [. . .] gathered our distant ancestors in unities inspired by the same spirit and by the same faith, but distributed with no effort in independent tribes and clans" (*ibid.*, 43). Thus, Marc traces elements of federalism in ancient Greece, in Rome, in the barbarian peoples, in feudalism and in the age of the Communes (Marc A., 1965, 4). The struggle between centralism and federalism is the same which in the past opposed the Celtic tribes to the Roman Empire (Aron R., Marc A., 1948, 43–44).

From this viewpoint, nationalism would be the result of "a wrong choice." The European states would have had the chance to organize themselves either in a federated or in a centralized form. In the context of a vision of history that neglects the conditioning by economic, political or juridical structures, the fact that nationalism and centralization have won would simply demonstrate that "the choice of the easiest road" prevailed (Aron R., Marc A., 1948, 20). Actually, the national state's democratic centralism was the means that allowed individuals to be freed from the old political and economic local institutions, in which the privileges of the old ruling classes of the feudal system were lurking. Compared to that system, democratic centralism was a progress: the premise for reconstructing regional and local autonomies in democratic terms. The supporters of federalism in a pre-national historical context (like the Girondists during the French Revolution) ended up being taken for the defenders of feudal particularism and from an objective standpoint they played a counter-revolutionary role.

According to Marc, federalism becomes self-conscious in the 19th century. Only then, thanks in particular to Proudhon's contribution, does integral federalism find its first theoretical formulation. It is a doctrine of a global character that covers a sphere larger than politics. It is "a philosophy that can put in touch again man with nature, the ego with the us, the man with his destiny, the man with his mystery. Philosophy, anthropology, sociology, law, political science: all is held together and federalism reveals itself capable of rejuvenating and renovating this 'whole'" (Aron R., Marc A., 1948, 6). At the heart of federalist philosophy there is the person. Against individualism the integral federalists set up personalism. "Federalism is a form of personalism" (Marc A., 1961, 35). By this expression Marc means that liberty and autonomy of a person can only be realized through personal relations, within communities of human dimensions of a territorial or professional character, and within the family.

The proposal to build a federalist society rests, according to this school of thought, on the application of four principles: autonomy, co-operation, participation and subsidiarity. The application of the autonomy principle to all territorial (communes, regions, etc.) and functional (the grass-root organizations of political parties, unions, enterprises, etc.) communities allows each community to self-rule, so that the decisions concerning the community are taken in accordance with the concrete needs of the individuals. The system of autonomies promotes the overcoming of the centralized and authoritarian model of the unitary state and makes it possible to reduce the role of central government. Co-operation among these communities allows them to avoid isolation and furthers the solution of common problems. The principle of participation makes it possible to introduce democracy within a plurality of autonomous communities, arranged at various levels and co-ordinated with each other, to which men belong and thus approach the ideal of a society in which men are masters of their destiny. The state, reduced to an executor of administrative-type functions, has to be subordinated to them; this implies a redistribution of the state's powers to the smaller territorial communities, applying the subsidiarity principle, according to which responsibilities have to be shared between the various government levels so as to assign them to the lowest level and to bring decisions as close as possible to the individual.

All the specific solutions are derived from these four principles. In contrast with the closed, centralized model of the unitary state, integral federalism emphasizes individuals' membership of a plurality of social groups, without anybody being privileged at the expense of others. In this respect, integral federalism's theoreticians criticize democratic centralism, as it allows people's participation in the decision-making process only through the channel of national parliaments, and the party system, which is eager to entrust a monopolistic representation of public opinion to professional politicians, who control closed, oligarchic and bureaucratic organizations.

Within this vision, there are differences between the various authors. For example, Marc stresses the role that the base cells of the federal system (the commune and the factory) must play for ensuring the direct participation of individuals in the political and economic life, and for freeing them from the power centres oppressing them. Others instead stress more the regional dimension, which may become a propulsive centre for a balanced and pluralistic development of the territory, and for the protection of ethnic and linguistic minorities. Among these authors there are some, for instance Jean-François Gravier (1915–2005), who recommend to give the greatest importance to the economic criterion in the definition of the regional borders to the detriment of the cultural and linguistic one, if necessary. It is to be pointed out that there is even an ethnic and linguistic variant of integral federalism, whose most notable figure is Guy Héraud (1920–2003). Finally, there is to mention that there are authors, like Robert Lafont (born in 1923) who think that it is possible to reconcile the economic and the ethnic criterion. Héraud believes that the regions' borders have to be drawn taking into account above all the ethnic criterion, in order to assure an effective autonomy to minorities. Such autonomy, however, must find a limitation in the federal order, a peaceful order ruled by law, which of course rules out secession. There is also a form of regionalism (Buchanan, 1994) for which self-government is not enough, but goes to the extreme of separatism. In this way, the notion of the region as an autonomous entity within a larger state unity is negated, and it is transformed in a closed-in group that develops the germ of racism and intolerance, reproducing in effect on a smaller scale the perversions and excesses of nationalism.

Mono-ethnic regions are, according to Héraud, more suitable than national states to become member-states of the European Union. This project, known as "Europe of the regions," supported also by Denis de Rougemont (1977, 336–338), who anyway did not agree with the exclusively ethnic definition of the region, would imply the suppression of national states once Europe's federative process will have reached its conclusion. To this proposal it has been objected that regions have insufficient dimensions and powers to be able to

push through any incisive initiative at the European level. A European federation composed of a mosaic of regional-dimension states, in which the national level is eliminated, would be doomed to oscillate between anarchy and
centralism. The most innovative aspect of the project of the European federation consists in reorganizing the state by establishing a new form of statehood, based on overcoming centralism and transferring powers upwards and
downwards. In this perspective the states will still keep a role: that of intermediate articulations between the regions and Europe. A national government
level will continue to be necessary not only for representing an efficient coun-
terweight to the European government, but also to solve the problems that
keep a national dimension, like those concerning national culture or the welfare state, which in the absence of a national government level would end up
falling under the competence of the European government (Rossolillo F., 58).

One of the most peculiar aspects of integral federalism is that it finds the
road to renewing democracy not only in power decentralization—whose essential aspects I have presented above—, but in organizing a new form of professional representation, in addition to the political one with a territorial base,
and, like it, structured at all levels, from the local to the European. This is the
corporative component of integral federalism, which, as the critics of this position have highlighted, instead of making democracy more embedded, would
end up creating more privileges. In fact, an assembly collecting the social and
economic interests would be the sum of particular wills, each tending to take
care of its interest in a unilateral and selfish fashion. As a consequence, it does
not constitute a remedy to the clash of corporate interests, because it is not
able to achieve mediation among the conflicting interests, nor a political syn-
thesis capable of letting the general will emerge.

The reform of the bicameral system proposed by Robert Aron and Alexandre Marc (1948, 108) grants to the chamber elected by universal suffrage the
function of controlling the executive branch, while to the second chamber,
composed of the representatives of the regional communities and of the economic and social interests, the legislative power is assigned. These considerations bring us to deal with the economic and social aspect of integral federalism, which places itself in opposition to both capitalism and collectivism.
Drawing inspiration from Proudhon, the integral federalists do not question
the principle of private property of the production means, although they think
that its distortions should be corrected. It is not possible, anyway, nor desir-
able, to abolish private property. Instead, it should be generalized. In agriculture they advocate co-operatives, in industry workers' participation in the
management of enterprises.

As far as planning is concerned, it must be rooted in the participation of regional and local bodies, of trade unions, of professional groups and enter-

prises, in granting autonomy, also financial, to each of these bodies, in their contractual co-operation and in a territorial distribution modelled on the federalist scheme of competence sharing. Moreover, planning operates through differentiated procedures: in the sector of vital needs (heavy industry, agriculture, housing, basic infrastructures, clothing, health, education) it has a mandatory character, while in the sector of consumers' goods and services it has an advisory character.

Two proposals aimed at furthering the democratization of the economy should be mentioned: the "guaranteed social minimum," which is a minimum income assuring to everybody the possibility to satisfy his essential needs, and the "civilian service," general and mandatory, which shares out to everybody the least qualified and unpleasant works not eliminated by automation, and makes it possible to finance with adequate resources the fund that assures the "guaranteed social minimum." The proposals presented by integral federalism in the economic field make up the guiding lines of a "third model," an idea that has recently received a growing interest by many quarters. However, the facets of the model, instead of being defined with relation to the developing trends of contemporary society, are derived in a doctrinarian fashion from the principles of federalism; this prevents its innovative aspects from being fully understood and assimilated.

Integral federalism had an original development in Italy in the thought of Adriano Olivetti (1901–1960), whose *L'ordine politico delle comunità (Political order of communities)*, published in 1945, is worth mentioning. At the heart of his political activity Olivetti places the community with a human dimension of 75,000–150,000 people, which, getting rid of the bureaucratic and authoritarian encrustations hampering democratic life, is where a direct and continuous participation of citizens to political life can take place. For strengthening democracy it is necessary to correct and integrate the universal suffrage, giving political voice to the forces of labour and culture. It is necessary then to give birth to institutions basing themselves, in addition to popular election, on requisites of technical and administrative competence. Thus, the General Council, the main decision-making body in the community, is composed for one third of representatives elected out of general political lists, for one third of representatives elected out of unions' lists and for one third designated by the forces of culture. The executive is organized according to seven political functions defining the essential tasks of a modern state: general affairs (with the task to regulate the relations among the state's bodies and to coordinate functions among them), justice, labour, health care, education, city-planning, social economy. To these functions correspond as many "departments," whose holders form the executive council of the community. The first two are elected by universal suffrage, the third and forth are elected by the workers, the fifth and sixth are appointed by open competition, the seventh is co-opted by the holders of the departments of general affairs, labour and education.

These functions represent a criterion for organizing the state vertically in "political orders." The members of the executive bodies of the various communities form the lower chamber of the region, and this elects out of its members the higher chamber. The national Parliament is composed of a Chamber of the communities, formed by all the members of the regional Senates, and of a Senate, which the orders contribute to form for one seventh each. The national executive is composed of the members of the regional executives. The purpose of this constitutional construction is to break up the particularism of both the smaller territorial communities and the economic and professional categories, in order to let the more general interests, coming from the larger territorial bodies, prevail. And at the same time it represents a method for selecting the political class, aiming to let climb to the top of the state the best people. There is to observe that, in tune with the federalist thinking, the constitutional pyramid devised by Olivetti does not stop at the national level, but can develop on the European and the world plane.

It is now possible to proceed to an overall evaluation of integral federalism. One must acknowledge its merit in having initiated a long time ago a severe criticism of the authoritarian aspects of the structure of the national state and of the ideology supporting it, and a reflection of a global character on federalism as an alternative to the crises of our time. Its most serious theoretical limit is not having paid sufficient interest to develop the conceptual tools necessary to interpret the objective course of history. And yet who chooses a political commitment must come to terms with the social, economic and political structures, seen as a set of objective conditions in which human behaviour is soaked, and which are not affected by our desires, however noble they are. A federalist commitment that does not want to limit itself to simply criticize reality (to negate it), but intends also to succeed in its concrete action to change the world, is obliged to never get detached from real processes of social and political life, but it must actively take part in them in order to know them and steer them. And this requires that some objectives internal to the current historical process and compatible with the historical conditions of our time be defined. In the case of integral federalism, the same criticism is applicable that Marx and Engels addressed to "utopian socialism," which, instead of looking in the historical process and its contradictions for the elements allowing one to assert the socialist alternative, was simply trusting to the force of ideas and to good will. Engels writes this about the founders of the socialist thought:

> The solution of the social problems, [. . .] the utopians attempted to evolve out
> of the human brain. Society presented nothing but wrongs; to remove these was
> the task of reason. It was necessary, then, to discover a new and more perfect

system of social order and to impose this upon society from without by propaganda, and, wherever it was possible, by the example of model experiments (Engels F., 1877, part III, I).

Like the utopian socialists, integral federalists conceive the federalist alternative as the total overturning of the social reality they fight. It is a position that limits itself to a simple negation, to an abstract refusal of that reality and to mechanically opposing utopia to reality. The objective of the federalist revolution, Marc writes, is "a radical remaking of all the structures [of society], be they social or political, economic or mental" (Marc A., 1965, 27). Thinking in terms of a global transformation of society means to dream of a project no revolutionary group has ever succeeded in materializing: to destroy this ill-done world and rebuild it from the foundations up.

Proudhon, the author the integral federalists draw inspiration from, had written to Antoine Gauthier: "You ask me to explain how to rebuild society [. . .]. It is not a matter of imagining, of putting together in our brains a system that later we will propose: you do not change the world like this. Society cannot correct itself but by itself" (Sainte-Beuve C.-A., 154). The problem is posed in clear terms. No political group can pretend to change society as a whole, nor, in any case, has the power to do so. Society changes through the behavior of all.

Nevertheless politics is that human activity which is entrusted with achieving self-government of society over itself by means of coercion and consent, two ingredients both indispensable and present, albeit in differing proportions, in every society that has existed so far. In politics there is always the imposition of a few (the governors) over the many (the governed). But historical experience demonstrates that political power does not last long without consent. In other words, it is not possible to make a policy prevail if this does not correspond to the needs of the people. It may thus be asserted that politics is the sphere where the revolutionary intervention of human action can change the course of events.

But it will simply be a matter of adjusting political institutions to the changes occurred in society. The revolutionary action never has the objective to radically transform society, but rather to break down the political institutions that are obstructing its development and hindering historical progress, and to create new institutions able to set free the trends come to maturity in society towards higher forms of political life.

The greatest difficulty of integral federalism has always been to define a political strategy. Although Olivetti's political project had worldwide dimensions, the Community Movement he founded in 1953 developed in Italy only, with the objective to reform the state's internal structures. The limit of this political vision lies in the Utopia of renovating the national state, a political formation which, due to its dimension and structure, is subordinate to political and economic international power centres, hence it is powerless for solving the fundamental problems of our time.

This is also the limit of the integral federalism component which developed in particular in France. The federalist alternative was conceived, due to the historical situation in which this movement developed, as a distant ultimate goal, which had no influence on the decisions of the moment. Even when, with the collapse of the national states in the second World War, the conditions matured for Europe's unification, they chose as their priority political objective to establish a federal society rather than to build a European federation. Sure enough, the supporters of integral federalism fought for the European federation within the Union of the European Federalists (founded in 1946), but their objective was above all the transformation of society in a federalist sense. As Marc stated: "A good constitution could only go alongside, be the expression, be the crowning of this necessary revolution, and not come before it or, so much the less, replace it" (Marc A., 1965, 27). Doubting that it was sufficient to fight for changing political institutions and that a European federation would have brought about a freer and more just society, they did not commit themselves enough in pursuing that objective and as a matter of fact they in the end accepted European unification policy pursued by the governments, which, by definition, does not question national sovereignty. This still is a widespread political attitude, which does not give to the federalist movement the responsibility of building the European unity, but expects such an outcome from the established authorities. And this is another trait in common with the utopian socialism.

As regards political efficiency, the definition of federalism as philosophy has had a negative role. In fact, those who, although sharing the political, economic and social goals of integral federalism, were totally or partly disagreeing with its philosophical formulation, distanced themselves from federalist commitment. That formulation should be in the sphere of personal choices, and not interfere with political stances. In conclusion, integral federalists have not been able to give a theoretical definition of federalism that could let it become the position of many, and turn it into a political force; that is to say, to form a nucleus of militants which would constitute the framework of an independent political organization, giving the other militants a theoretical guidance and motivating their political commitment. The Italian federalism has the merit to have overcome these limits.

7. 3 FEDERALISM AS IDEOLOGY

The conception of federalism as an independent ideology is the most innovative aspect of Italian federalism. It is a line of thought which asserts the topical relevance of the federalist alternative and bases it on a peculiar analysis of the fundamental trends of contemporary history.

The starting point of this new approach can be placed in the thinking of Carlo Rosselli (1899–1937), an anti-fascist exile in France, murdered with his brother Nello (1900–1937) by hired fascist assassins in 1937, who came to the conclusion that the only real alternative to fascism was represented by the United States of Europe. After Hitler's victory in Germany, fascism revealed its nature of a Europe-wide phenomenon. With astonishing clear-sightedness Carlo Rosselli in 1933 understood that "fascism [. . .] has won" (Rosselli C., 205, vol. 2), and that its victory required that the resistance be organized on a European level around a European left, with the support of the big democratic powers: France and Great Britain. To the anti-fascists, who were just advocating the restoration of the democratic method as the objective around which the fight for overthrowing fascism should be organized, Rosselli objects that a European phenomenon cannot be defeated on a national plane, and opposes to that the great idea of the United States of Europe. Rosselli's perception is in harsh contrast with the recurring illusion by the democratic and socialist movements, who use to make up some convenient enemy in their national context, easier to fight, but whose international ties they choose to ignore.

But it is not only for this judgment that Carlo Rosselli proves to be the highest conscience of the *Giustizia e Libertà (Justice and Liberty)*, a liberal-socialist movement, which advocated democratic and liberal political institutions, a mixed economy, social justice and international peace. With an acute perception, forerunning the developments of the federalist strategy after the war, he writes in 1935: "There is no other foreign policy for the European left! The United States of Europe, the European Assembly. The rest is *flatus vocis*, the rest is catastrophe." Thus he formulates the strategic objective whoever wants to "make Europe" must pursue:

> To plan [. . .] from this very moment the meeting of a *European Assembly*, composed of delegates elected *by the peoples*, that in absolute parity of rights and duties drafts the first *European Federal Constitution*, appoints the first *European Government*, sets the fundamental principles of a *European coexistence*, organizes a force at the service of the new European laws and gives birth to the United States of Europe (Rosselli C., 205, vol. 2).

But, at the time, the first political priority was the defeat of Fascism and Nazism. Thus, that bald design was only an anticipation of a political goal which will be pursued after the Second World War. In the third issue of *L'unità europea (The European Unity)*, the journal of the European Federalist Movement in Italy, published in September 1943, there was an anonymous editorial, attributed to Ernesto Rossi, entitled "War to Nazism." According to the American historian Charles Delzell, it is the first antifascist document urging the armed struggle against Fascism and Nazism (Delzell C.F., 241–250).

The writings that Einaudi, under the pen-name of Junius, collected in 1920 in the booklet titled *Political Letters,* had no influence whatsoever on the political and cultural debate of the immediate post-war period, and were forgotten by the author himself. When, during the Second World War, that book happened to fall into the hands of two anti-fascists, Altiero Spinelli (1907–1986) and Ernesto Rossi (1897–1967), interned at Ventotene, a small island in the Tyrrhenian sea off the coast between Rome and Naples, it appeared to them as a revelation. Those pages represented the starting point of the reflections that led to the drafting of the *Ventotene Manifesto* in 1941, which represents a veritable turning point in federalist literature: the passing from theoretical reflection to a program of action.

When Spinelli was arrested and then convicted by the fascist special tribunal in 1927, he was just twenty years old and was a leader of the young communists. His solitary reflections in jail led him to choose the value of freedom and to give up communism in 1937. The choice of democracy represented for Spinelli only the beginning of a difficult intellectual journey. The encounter in 1939 at Ventotene with Ernesto Rossi, one of the leaders of the movement "Giustizia e Libertà," marked Spinelli for life. Rossi was the vehicle of federalist culture. As a professor of economics, he was authorized to correspond with Einaudi, who sent him some books by Lionel Robbins.

The concept of crisis of the national state, that allows us to see contemporary history in a new perspective, made it possible for Spinelli to analyse in depth the causes of imperialism and fascism, whose essential elements were already present in the works of his mentors. At the root of these phenomena there is the fusion of state and nation, which creates an explosive mixture and gives rise to authoritarian trends within the state and to aggressive trends in the international plane. Ultimately, the cause of imperialism and war lies in state sovereignty and international anarchy. The more specific cause of imperialism in the era of the world wars is to be found in the crisis of the European system of states. It was brought about by the internationalization of the productive process, which pushed every state to try to weaken its neighbours through protectionism and to enlarge the economic space under the control of each of them, driving Germany to wage war for getting hegemony over the whole continent.

As far as fascism is concerned, it is the point of arrival of the historical evolution of the national state, the expression of the belligerent and authoritarian trends dormant in its closed and centralized structure and become virulent with the exacerbation of power contest in Europe. On the economic and social plane, fascism is seen as the totalitarian and corporatist answer to the economic stagnation of a market whose dimensions are inadequate for the development of modern production techniques; an answer to the disintegration of society, which is reduced to a battle-ground among corporate interests; to the need to eliminate social divisions, which make weaker the State's capability to defend itself; and to the need to adjust the production system to the requirements of a war economy.

But Spinelli's work takes on a truly innovative significance in the field of action. Federalism assumes the character of a criterion for understanding and action, inspiring a new political behaviour and an autonomous political struggle. In this perspective, Spinelli has laid the premises for arriving at a definition of federalism as ideology, even if he has always refused to agree with this view (Spinelli A., 1960, 15), mostly in order to mark the difference between his position and that of integral federalists. Actually, with his work he has contributed to advance the theoretical and practical autonomy of federalism more than any other federalist has ever done. He considers the European Federation as a true political alternative to the system of national states, and as the priority objective of a new political program, which is taken as its own by a new movement, organized for the sole purpose to pursue that objective.

Spinelli advanced on the new road that Einaudi started to tread. The longer we observe Spinelli's activities after his release from confinement, the more evident becomes the distance which separates him from Einaudi, whose little book written twenty years earlier had revealed the main features of federalist theory. Two major limits of Einaudi's federalism may be highlighted.

First of all, for Einaudi federalism remained an idea ancillary to liberalism, a simple institutional scheme able to protect the democratic and liberal values and institutions from the consequences of international anarchy. Federalism is "a canon for the interpretation of politics" (Spinelli A., 1989, 214, vol. 1). In a passage of his diary Spinelli enunciates this important definition of federalism. The adoption of this point of view enables us to distinguish also Spinelli's from Rossi's approach to federalism. In Spinelli's opinion, Rossi "did not even suspect" (Spinelli A., 1989, 214, vol. 1) that this could be the nature of federalism. Rossi conceives federalism simply as a method for the organization of power, a constitutional technique which abolishes armed conflicts among states which have subscribed to a federal pact. In other words, federation appears as an alternative to war and not the response to the main problems of the current phase of history characterized by the historical crisis of the nation-state. Conceived in these terms, federalism is simply the completion of liberalism and socialism. In comparison with Spinelli, Rossi's (and Einaudi's) adherence to federalism had a weaker motivation.

Moreover, in Einaudi's works no political proposal on how to carry out the federalist design can be found. Once he had illustrated the nature of the objective to be pursued, he considered his task accomplished. After all, this was also the limit to Rossi's political outlook. Anybody who reads his most important essay on European federalism, *Gli Stati Uniti d'Europa* (*The United States of Europe*), published in Switzerland under the pen name of Storeno in 1944, can remark that his masterly illustration of the historical and political reasons for European unification is not associated with any reflection on the action which is necessary to pursue that objective. All this explains why Rossi, who had been one of the founders of the *Movimento Federalista Europeo* (*European Federalist Movement*), abandoned his federalist commitment after the fall of the European Defence Community in 1954, when, owing to the thawing of the Cold War, the danger of a Third World War began to lessen.

Spinelli developed a new sector of federalist thinking: the theory of a democratic action for unifying a group of states. I resume here its main aspects.

a) Spinelli differentiates himself from those who before him chose federalism for expressing their political position, but limited themselves to denounce the historical crisis of the national state without proposing a precise action program, and placing the European federation in an undefined future. Spinelli's political vision rests on a central idea, the one of the topical importance of the European federation, a political objective that is not only necessary, but has also become possible in the new historical context created by the Second World War. Spinelli's forecast was that the war would bring to maturity the objective conditions for Europe's unification, making the crisis of the national state evolve in a political crisis, and would thus open the road to the federalist initiative.

> The ideal of a European federation, a prelude to a world federation—the Eugenio Colorni's *Preface* to *The Ventotene Manifesto* reads—while it might have been considered a distant utopia a few years ago, seems now to be, at the end of this war, an attainable goal, almost within our reach. The European federation, seen as a stage on the road to a world federation, is the objective of an immediate and concrete battle, guided by a movement expressly created to lead that battle (Spinelli A., Rossi E., 1988, 14).

b) The second novelty consists in the strategic priority given to the goal of the European federation, over that of the renovation of the national state. What the parties of liberal, democratic, socialist and national ideologies have in common is the priority they give to the betterment of their state and their belief that peace is the automatic consequence of the establishment of the principles of, respectively, liberty, equality, social justice and national independence. The peculiarity of the federalist viewpoint consists in the over-turning of this priority.

> The question that must be resolved first, failing which progress is no more than mere appearance, is the definitive abolition of the division of Europe into national, sovereign states [. . .]. Anyone taking the problem of the international order as the central problem in this historical age, and considering its solution to be the prerequisite for solving all the institutional, economic and social problems imposed on our society, is obliged to consider all the issues relating to internal political contrasts and the attitudes of each political party from this point of view, even with regard to the tactics and strategies of daily struggle (Spinelli A., Rossi E., 1988, 31, 13).

Who attends only to national renovation does not act upon the cause of international conflicts, imperialism and war. Due to international anarchy, national independence tends to turn into nationalism, liberty tends to be sacrificed to the need to centralize power and favor military security; military expenses are an alternative to social expenses. Unlike political parties (and traditional ideologies inspiring them) which generally continue to confine themselves to plan government or regime changes within state borders, but do not question their own state, the federalist project aims at a more radical change, which affects the very nature of the state, i.e. its transformation into a member state of a federation. For Spinelli, federalism is the response to the greatest problems of contemporary society, which have acquired much wider dimensions than nation-states. The federalist outlook is the expression of the awareness that the European unification and the unification of other great regions of the world in the perspective of world unity, have the priority over the goal of renewing individual states considered separately

All this highlights the lack of autonomy of internal politics and the illusion of the reform of the national state, by now surpassed by processes transcending it. Therefore, "if tomorrow the struggle were to remain restricted within traditional national boundaries, it would be very difficult to avoid the old contradictions" (Spinelli A., Rossi E., 1988, 29). Since the traditional political forces pursue the reform of the national State, they remain prisoners of that institution, suffer from its decline and hence place themselves in the camp of conservatism.

c) From the above it ensues, therefore, a shifting of the centre of political struggle from the national plane to the international. A new dividing line tends to be established between the forces of progress and those of conservatism:

> Therefore, the dividing line between progressive and reactionary parties no longer coincides with the formal lines of more or less democracy, or the pursuit

of more or less socialism, but the division falls along a very new and substantial line: those who conceive the essential scope and goal of struggle as being the ancient one, the conquest of national political power, and who, albeit involuntarily, play into the hands of reactionary forces, letting the incandescent lava of popular passions set in the old moulds, and thus allowing old absurdities to arise once again, and those who see the main purpose as the creation of a solid international state, who will direct popular forces towards this goal, and who, even if they were to win national power, would use it first and foremost as an instrument for achieving international unity (Spinelli A., Rossi E., 1988, 32–33).

In the era of the crisis of the national state and of the internationalisation of the productive process, the clash between the forces of progress and those of conservatism takes no longer place in the national arena between the principles of liberty and dictatorship, or between those of socialism and capitalism. Who chooses to commit himself in the national plane, even if his objective is to realize more democracy or more socialism, places himself in the camp of conservatism, because his political action consolidates the national states. As a consequence, the objective to pursue above all by those willing to promote progress is the overcoming of the division of Europe and of the world in sovereign states. The supranational era makes a new dividing line emerge among the political and social forces: that between nationalism and federalism.

d) To be able to pursue their objectives independently of governments and political parties, federalists had to have their own organization. The authors of *The Ventotene Manifesto* felt that this organization should be the party and more precisely a revolutionary party. This was a survival of Leninist culture, which had influenced Spinelli's political education and was soon amended. The Italian federalist organization, whose foundation was promoted by Spinelli in Milan on 27–28 August 1943, took the shape of the political movement and an analogous structure was adopted by the federalist organizations in the other countries of Europe partly because of the influence of the Italian federalists. The fact is that the struggle for national power would have strengthened this power and hence consolidated the division of Europe, whereas the organization as a movement made it possible to unite forces favourable to the European constitutional objective not only over and above party divisions, but also over and above national divisions.

Spinelli and Rossi had come to the belief that the resistance movements all over Europe would have drawn the same lessons from the war and they would have then proposed similar projects for reorganizing Europe in unitary terms. Their release from internment following Benito Mussolini's fall let the two authors of the *Ventotene Manifesto* expatriate to Switzerland in the fall of

1943, just after they founded the *Movimento Federalista Europeo (European Federalist Movement)* in Italy. There, they got in contact with the other resistance movements.

The Ventotene program was recognized as the most radical, but also the most advanced and comprehensive vision of European unity. It inspired the declaration of the Resistance fighters (*L'Europe de demain*, 68–75) by nine countries in July 1944, which was distributed among the resistance movements all over Europe. The document clearly illustrates the need to abandon the dogma of national sovereignty and defines the European federation as the condition for any progress. That meeting was the first step on the road towards the establishment of a federalist movement on the European level, which will take place in 1946. The movement (the *European Union of Federalists*) was the necessary tool for transcending national borders, inside which political struggle had remained confined.

The federalist struggle does not make use of the same instruments and procedures as normal policy-makers (the political parties and the governments) do, because its objective is not the conquest of an already existing power, but the creation of a new power. The obstacle to surmount is the resistance the holders of national sovereignty oppose to transferring power to the European level, even if it is not possible to proceed on the road to the European federation without the agreement of the governments. Hence the necessity to use a political instrument, like the federalist movement, not directly involved in the national political struggle, with the aim to push governments to cede part of their power when the opportunity arises.

e) When the war ended, while the governments were rebuilding the national States, but simultaneously were promoting European integration with the instruments of foreign policy, Spinelli started off a democratic struggle of a constituent character for European unity. From the experience of the birth of the United States and in the wake of Carlo Rosselli's perception, Spinelli understood that the constituent method was the only procedure possible for bringing to conclusion the building of a democratic power in Europe. On the one hand, a European constituent assembly, representing all of the peoples and political forces in Europe, is the only body entitled to act with the legitimation deriving to it from the vote, and is therefore provided with the authority necessary to draft and propose a Constitution. On the other, in a democratic assembly decisions are taken publicly and by a majority vote, with procedures that allow to clearly see responsibilities and to come to democratic and productive decisions: the opposite of the diplomatic method, which is based on the principle of decisions taken in secrecy and by unanimity, requires that national sovereignty is not to be hurt and drives to compromises that have to take into account the interests of all of the states.

The operating method illustrated above was followed by Spinelli in two attempts at building a European federation.

The first took place between 1951 and 1954, when, under the pressure of cold war, the United States and Great Britain proposed to give back to Western Germany a full economic and military sovereignty, and the French government, faced with the prospect of a revival of German nationalism, accepted Jean Monnet's suggestion to subject to a European authority the two pillars of Germany's power: the coal and steel industry and the army. Thus the European Coal and Steel Community (ECSC) was created and the European Defence Community (EDC) was started up. Spinelli denounced the contradiction of an army without a government. With the help of the Italian Premier Alcide De Gasperi (1881–1954), of whom he won the agreement, he succeeded in getting the decision that to the ECSC Parliamentary Assembly (which was given the name of *ad hoc* Assembly) the mandate be assigned to draft a Constitution of the European Political Community, the political body with a democratic basis to which the task had to be awarded to exercise the control of the European army.

Although in the project prepared by the *ad hoc* Assembly there was not a clear choice between confederation and federation, the political European Community had a strong evolutionary potential to become a federation. The direct election of the Chamber of the Peoples would have created a power centre with an interest to complete the democratisation of the Community and to extend its powers from the military to the economic and monetary sectors. But the ratification process of the draft treaty was suddenly stopped on August 30th, 1954, when the French National Assembly rejected it after four out of six members of the European Community had already approved it. After Stalin's death, the international situation had changed: the need for a European defensive system appeared less stringent. Thus, the first attempt to establish a European state failed.

The fall of the EDC was a big defeat for the federalists. However, it did not eliminate the historical trend towards European unification, and the energies that the action for creating the European Political Community had aroused constituted the base for relaunching the integration process. The political choice that inspired the institution of the European Economic Community in 1957 was to make the European integration proceed in the economic field, that is, along the line of least resistance, so as to avoid the stumbling-block of ceding sovereignty to supra-national institutions. The institutions which have to set the guiding-lines of the Community's policies and of those for building the European unity, are transitional institutions, which have to manage the passage of Western Europe from division to unity. It is to be noted that it would be incorrect to simply define the Community as a confederation. Its peculiarity is that its institutional order is the result of an interlacement of confederal and federal thrusts. It compounds the defence of national interests and the necessity to take decisions in common, which represents the typical aspect of confederations. But at the same time it has been devised so as to adapt itself to the step by step nature of the unification process, which, by creating an ever deeper "*de facto* solidarity" (Monnet J., 300), subjects to a permanent tension the Community institutions and makes them evolve up to the goal of a federal union. The history of European unification shows that the federation cannot be made by one big leap. "Europe will not be built all at once, or as a single whole," Monnet said (Monnet J., 300). It is a process that progresses through a series of successive constitutional acts, which, for some aspects, may be compared to the formation of the modern state.

Let us consider a little closer the two models for approaching Europe's unification project: functionalism and constitutionalism. The functionalist approach is a method that allows for partial sectors to be integrated in order to create a *de facto* solidarity among the States and to make ceding sovereignty easier. The constitutional approach suggests, instead, to squarely confront the problem of creating an irrevocable system of federal government. Historical experience has shown that the functionalist strategy has made it possible to initiate, but not to bring to conclusion, European unification. The conclusion of the process requires a mobilization of a constituent power and a constitutional solution. Therefore, the two approaches can be considered complementary: Monnet's has allowed him to initiate the process of European integration, Spinelli's is indispensable for bringing it to conclusion.

The second attempt at constructing the European federation was promoted by Spinelli in the European Parliament after its direct election. The draft Treaty on the establishment of a European Union, approved by the European Parliament in 1984, even if it was not a perfect federal constitution, contained the elements which would have favoured an evolution in a federal sense of European institutions: extension of the Community competences in the direction of an economic and monetary Union and of a political Union; transformation of the Council into the Chamber of the States, which was sharing with the European Parliament the legislative power; granting to the Commission the role of government, accountable to the Parliament. The contradiction of a Parliament elected by universal suffrage but provided with a consultative power only, allowed to open the battle for awarding the power to make laws and to control the executive to the sovereign people, through its Parliamentary representation. This attempt failed, due to the opposition of the United Kingdom, which was only willing to accept a more limited objective: the completion of the internal market by 1992; this was decided with the approval of the Single European Act (1986).

But a market cannot function without a currency and without a government. With the Maastricht Treaty the decision was taken to institute a single currency and a European Central Bank by 1999. The Treaties of Amsterdam (1997) and Nice (2000), albeit reinforcing the Parliament's legislative and control powers, did not eliminate the democratic deficit of the Union, nor did they transfer to it the necessary powers for speaking with one voice in the sectors of foreign, security and defense policy. A Charter of Fundamental Rights of the European Union has been proclaimed in Nice on 7 December 2000 and a European Constitution has been signed by the 25 member states of the EU on 29 October 2004. But he rejection of the latter in France and the Netherlands has prevented it from coming into force. This shows the negative consequence of the veto, which the Constitution maintains in the fields of foreign, security and fiscal policies and the constitutional revision. This is at variance with the democratic principle and enables the will of a small minority to prevail over that of the majority.

In conclusion, in order to measure the progress achieved by the federalist project it is sufficient to compare the maturity level reached so far by the European unification process with the moment when, after having been freed from his internment in Ventotene, Spinelli initiated his plan of action. At that time Spinelli was alone with his ideas and there was nothing above the States. Approximately seventy years after *The Ventotene Manifesto* and half century after the establishment of the European Community, we have to acknowledge that Spinelli had rightly interpreted the new direction that the historical process would have taken. At the beginning, the EC was a union of six countries. Now it stretches from Lapland to the Mediterranean and from Poland to the Canaries and includes 27 countries. It is a Community of 487 million inhabitants, where 23 official languages are spoken and includes approximately 100 ancient ethnic minorities. It has an executive commission, a parliament directly elected with legislative powers, a chamber of states, a court of justice, a central bank, a currency, a citizenship, a flag, an anthem, a passport. National borders have been abolished. The unification process has developed with the ups and downs characteristic of a difficult undertaking such as the overcoming of the sovereignty of an increasing number of states which joined the original core of the founding states. But the fact remains that the most important achievement of the EU is undoubtedly peace. After centuries of warfare, Europe has never before lived so long in peace as it now has in the post-2nd World War period which coincides with the beginning of the process of European unification.

Of course, although it is being realized through successive gradual transformations, Spinelli's project remains still unaccomplished. But the proof of the validity of his vision lies in the efficacy of the action he has inspired, in the agreement between events and his design.

Despite he devoted his best energies for about fifty years to European uni-fication, what Spinelli neglected is federalist theory, that he believed it was possible to find ready-made in the federalist literature. Thus he did not feel the need to rethink it and make it more comprehensive, adjusting it to the new challenges of contemporary history. Mario Albertini is the one who gave the most innovative contribution in that area. He started to work out a scientific critique of the idea of nation, which could lead to a radical negation of the na-tional system and to the building of a theory of federalism seen no longer as a constitutional technique, able to make a peaceful coexistence of a set of in-dependent and coordinated governments possible, but as an ideology high-lighting the sense of the course of history in our epoch.

When Albertini tackled the problem of defining the notion of federalism, he came up against the shortcomings of current definitions which limited themselves to the institutional aspect, and he felt the need to develop a more comprehensive theory that would distinguish the value aspect from the struc-tural and historical-social aspect. Albertini contended that such an analytical approach was applicable to all ideologies (Albertini M., 1993, 91). The value aspect defines the goal pursued by the ideology. The structural aspect ex-plores the way power must be organized to achieve the goal. The historical-social aspect defines the historical context within which it is possible to real-ize a value through the appropriate power structure.

Viewed from this standpoint, federalism becomes a far vaster subject than that covered by the theory of federal institutions. Yet even today, in the wake of *The Federalist*, many scholars continue to cultivate a narrow approach. In his book on federalism, Albertini remarks that the institutions are conditioned by society, which represents the infrastructure of the institutions, and the lat-ter, in turn, constitute governmental tools for generating political decisions and thus pursuing specific values. Therefore, any comprehensive definition of federalism demands that alongside the institutional aspect, should also con-sider the historical-social aspect and the value aspect. If all three elements are taken into account, federalism becomes an ideology that has a structure (the federal state), value (peace) and an historical and social aspect (the overcom-ing of society's division into classes and nations). The value aspect of feder-alism is peace. Federalism is to peace what liberalism is to freedom, democ-racy to equality and socialism to social justice.

In this respect, Albertini shares Kant's political, juridical and philosophi-cal-historical standpoint, which has been put at the top of the political agenda by the crisis of the national state and the expansion—across borders—of the interdependence of human action, of which European unification is the most highly developed embodiment. These phenomena should be regarded as the premises for perpetual peace through the construction of a world federation. Denying the nation, with European federation, means denying "the culture that fosters the political division of the human kind" and at the same time, affirming "within nations [a] truly human [. . .] multinational model, [. . .] the political culture of the unity of the human kind" (Albertini M., 1993, 288–289). World wars and the nuclear weaponry would seem to suggest that Kant was correct when he predicted that it is only by experiencing the destructiveness of war that states would relinquish their 'savage freedom' and bow to a common law.

The structural aspect of federalism lies in the federal state, which promotes the overcoming of the closed and centralized structures of the national state with the formation, downstream, of genuine regional and local autonomies, and the realization, upstream, of effective forms of political and social solidarity, above and beyond national states.

The historical and social aspect of federalism consists in overcoming the division of the human kind into rival classes and nations: only thus can pluralism develop that is typical of a federal society, and is expressed by the principle of unity in diversity. In federal societies, there is a level playing field in which loyalty towards the overall society actually coexists with loyalty towards smaller local communities—regions, provinces, cities, neighbourhoods and so on. But this social balance has developed only partially in past federal societies, because on the one hand class struggle has made the sense of belonging to a class prevail over all other forms of social solidarity and prevented strong bonds of solidarity from taking root in regional and local communities, and on the other, the struggle between states at the international level has strengthened the central authority at the expense of local powers.

The notion of federalism as an ideology does not just highlight the limitations of the reductionist approach, which defines federalism as merely a constitutional technique (K.C. Wheare). Albertini's critique is addressed also to such visions as the integral federalism of Alexandre Marc or Denis de Rougemont and that of Daniel Elazar, which define federalism as unity in diversity. Albertini calls this a generic and historically indeterminate concept, which traces the roots of federalism back to the dim and distant past, when the first forms of association emerged between tribes, and detects traces of it in all eras, from the leagues between the free cities of ancient Greece, to the Roman Empire, the city-republics of medieval Italy and Germany, the Holy Roman Empire and so on. The concept elaborated by Albertini, instead, has major consequences on the periodization of federalism. In his view, representative democracy constitutes an essential requirement for federal institutions. The outcome of this assumption is that the United States of America represent the archetypal federation. Hence it is not possible to class as federal any of the earlier political formations listed above: though they feature an institutional framework based on the decentralization of power, nonetheless they did not have a democratic structure. At most they can be classified as the precursors of federalism.

In keeping with the above definition, Albertini divided the development of federalist thinking into three phases. The first phase, going from the French Revolution to the first world war, is characterized by the emergence, still only in principle, of the community and cosmopolitan component of federalism, opposed to the authoritarian and warlike aspects of the national state. The second phase is the period between the two world wars, when the criteria of federalism were resorted to to interpret the crisis of the national state and the European states system. The first phase began after the second world war and is still ongoing: in this phase the conceptual schemes and political and institutional tools of federalism are necessary for resolving the crisis of Europe.

It is easier to understand the significance of federalism if one starts looking at it from the point of view of what it negates, rather than what it affirms. In point of fact, the positive determinations of federalist theory have gradually become clear through the experience of refusing both the division of the mankind into sovereign states and the centralization of political power. Since these phenomena have appeared most distinctly in the Europe of nations, federalism has primarily cast itself as the *negation of the national state*.

The first task of Albertini's research programme was to elaborate a theory of the nation (Albertini M., 1997). His aim was to tear apart the nation-centric paradigm of politics, which is the embodiment of an archaic culture unable to deal with the major issues of the contemporary world. The method used by Albertini was to define the nation on the basis of the empirical observation of human behaviour. The national behaviour is a behaviour of loyalty; its objective landmark is the state, which is regarded not as such, but rather as an illusory entity linked to cultural, aesthetic, sporting experiences whose specific nature is not national. Albertini wonders why an Italian, admiring the Gulf of Naples, claims that: 'Italy is beautiful'. At the heart of this statement lies a political phenomenon. When people attend national schools, celebrate national holidays, pay national taxes, and are conscripted into the national armed forces to be trained to kill and be killed for the nation, they express these behaviours in terms of loyalty to a mythical entity, the nation, an idealized representation of the bureaucratic and centralized states. Such an idealization of reality is the mental reflection of relations of power between individuals and the national state.

In *Lo stato nazionale* (*The National State*) he defined the nation as the ideological reflection of people's belonging to a certain type of state: the bureaucratic centralized state. This political formation, typical of the European continent, requires an integration of citizens in the state, the more strong the more power is centralized, so as to subject the country's material and ideal resources to the direct control of the central government. Whilst in the British isle, instead, power decentralization has made possible the coexistence of the British, Welsh and Scottish nations. A national conscience, as a wide-spread fact in the population, is then the consequence (and not the premise) of the formation of the national state and of a precise political program, worked out for the first time by the Jacobins during the French Revolution, whose purpose was to impose a unity of language, culture and traditions over the whole state territory. This brought with it the destruction of all spontaneous nationalities (nations in the etymological sense of the word, that is, the territory where individuals are born (lat. *natus,* (pl.) *nati*) and live), and the transferring to the state plane of the feelings of affection and belonging that people have always had towards their natural community. The fusion of state and nation became then for national governments the basis for exacting by their citizens an exclusive loyalty and for adopting an aggressive foreign policy.

Albertini stretched the notion of ideology, which Marx had restricted to class positions, to include relations of power within the state. On this basis it is possible to demystify the idea of nation, which started out originally as a revolutionary idea and today has become an element of conservatism. Insofar as it depicts the political division between nations as something right and natural, even sacred, it opposes the basic trend of contemporary history towards the internationalization of the productive process, which demands that the state should organize itself on a vast political space along multinational and federal lines.

Federalism's negation of the national state appeared as far back as the French Revolution, when nationalism was also in its infancy, but initially and for quite some time emphasis was placed on principles and values. At that time, the conditions had not yet arisen for federalism to represent a viable political alternative to the organization of Europe into national states, and foster political action. However, the roots of federalism's opposition to the system of national states were deep. It is unreasonable to regard the liberal, democratic and socialist values that in the 19th century brought about new models of political coexistence, but were only partially and precariously realized within national states, as limited only to the national arena. On the other hand, the extension of those values to Europe as a whole, as a pathway to universal application, is impossible without employing federal institutions.

The situation changed with the coming of the industrial society—specifically the second phase of the industrialization process that 'increases the intensity and frequency of relations between the individuals belonging to different states, expanding the sphere of international politics' (Albertini M., 1993, 147). A new phenomenon now begins to emerge: *the crisis of the national state* (Albertini M., 1993, chapt. 4), the concept on which the theoretical autonomy of contemporary federalism is founded. This concept matches what liberal thought calls the crisis of the *ancien régime*, and socialism and communism call the crisis of capitalism; and through it, the basic contradiction of an entire era can be detected, and a global historical assessment formulated. It is the concept that both Trotsky and Einaudi employed to explain World War One. German imperialism is seen as the negative expression of Europe's need for unity. The alternative to a Europe unified by violence is represented for both by the United States of Europe. But only after the second world war did the issue of European unity acquire a political nature. The process of European integration represents the historical issue that lies at the heart of Albertini's theoretical elaboration. He devised an impressive amount of analytical categories which, together, constitute the complex conceptual framework needed to master the process both theoretically and practically. There is too little space here to illustrate the many relevant aspects, so I will simply provide the main features of Albertini's interpretation.

In the period following the second world war, the national states were "no longer able on their own to fulfil the two fundamental tasks of any state: economic development and the defence of their citizens." Hence the crisis of consent towards national institutions. National governments were consequently "permanently faced with the choice of 'divided we fall, united we stand' [. . .] Their very *raisons d'état* gives them no other option than to resolve their problems jointly" (Albertini M., 1999, 237).

In 1968 Albertini reached the conclusion the European integration had become "irreversible." His argument goes like this:

Integration among the Six is merely the most advanced stage of a vaster process of integration that looks like the beginning of a new historical cycle, promoted by an irresistible historical force. Such an evolution obviously does not rule out the possibility of crisis or even of periods of stagnation and involution, which might even affect the Common Market itself. But in principle it does rule out the possibility of a stable return to a closed market system. [He concludes that the irreversibility of the process depends] on the evolution of the mode of production, i.e. on a primary historical factor (Albertini M., 1999, 256).

Albertini dedicated much of his intellectual energy to studying European unification, which he viewed as the foremost expression of the supranational course of history. Federalism is the formula that enables this process to be understood and controlled. Federalism today has a role comparable to what liberalism, democracy and socialism were in the past: through the development and dissemination of the culture of peace, federalism propounds a society capable of resolving the critical issues of our time; it reopens the possibility of thinking of the future, which was overshadowed in traditional ideologies because of the exhaustion of their revolutionary thrust.

However, to rise to this challenge, federalism must renew itself, elaborate new categories of analysis, and invent new institutional formulas. It asserts that it is "a new world, which men and women will learn to understand as they create it" (Albertini M., 1999, 161–162). European Federation represents thus the crucial event of our time, the first real federal unification ever achieved, insofar as it will unite historically consolidated nations. It will represent a milestone in our history, the beginning of the unification of the human kind. In contrast, the significance of all the Federations that have existed until now was that of having created a new state in a world divided into states, in which the political division of mankind seemed to be an insurmountable condition.

European Federation will arise

> from the negation of the political division of the human kind. This is, historically, the most important thing—according to Albertini. National culture, conceived as the theory of the political division of the human kind, is one which by mystifying liberalism, democracy and socialism—soviet or otherwise—legitimated the duty to kill. A duty negated by a culture that historically negates the political division of the human kind. It is a vindication in the sphere of thought of the political—not just the spiritual—right not to kill, and hence the historical framework for the struggle to affirm this right in practice, above and beyond European Federation, with the world federation' (Albertini M., 1999, 135).

As we have seen, the goal of peace defines federalism as an independent ideology. The approach to the issue of peace and war defines the main difference separating federalism from other ideologies.

When the theorists of liberalism, democracy and socialism looked at the future of international relations, they imagined that people, unshackled from the domination of the monarchy, the aristocracy, the bourgeoisie and capitalism and as such, masters of their fate, would no longer resort to war. In short, it can be stated that liberalism, democracy and socialism share a common view of international politics, a view defined as internationalism: they interpret international politics using the same categories with which they explain domestic politics; they attribute international tensions and wars exclusively to the nature of the internal structures of states; and they consider peace as the automatic and necessary consequence of the transformation of the internal structures of states. Thus, internationalism is a political conception which in theory does not attribute any autonomy to the international political system with respect to the internal structure of individual states, or to foreign policy with respect to domestic policy; and in practice prioritizes the spread of freedom and equality within the individual states, at the expense of achieving peace and international order.

As Kant put it, peace becomes possible only if the states that join the world federation have a republican constitution, in which each citizen accepts limitations to the exercise of their freedom, by obeying a common set of laws which everyone else is also willing to respect, having together contributed to drafting it. In other words, freedom and equality are not vehicles of peace but merely "premises for peace" (Albertini M., 1993, 42–43). The fulfilment of these principles allows for the achievement of a form of civil coexistence, featuring peaceable relations between individuals, i.e. social peace. And social peace must be regarded as a requirement for international peace. On the other hand, the decision to join the Federation must be a free choice: this is the difference between Federation and Empire.

Conversely, federalism considers international anarchy as a hindrance to consolidating freedom, democracy and social justice within states, and sees peace—the creation of an international juridical order—as the condition for defeating the warlike and authoritarian tendencies always simmering under the surface of the state. This viewpoint is a radical reversal of the prevalent thinking among followers of liberalism, democracy and socialism, who still today place the reform of the state above the achievement of international order, and delude themselves that peace will automatically flow from the dissemination of liberal, democratic and socialist principles within the individual states. So a clear-cut but generally unrecognized criterion is identified, which explains not only the reason why the dissemination of liberal, democratic and socialist principles has failed to usher in an era of peace, but also why these principles have taken such an incomplete and precarious foothold in a world of clashing sovereign states.

In conclusion, to quote Albertini's formula, "whilst the *historical affirmation* of each of these ideologies constitutes one of the premises for peace, peace conceived as world government is the necessary premise for their *complete realization*, proving immediately that peace cannot be built by simply reinforcing these ideologies" (Albertini, 1999, 171).

Accordingly, federalism does not compete with the other ideologies, but complements them. This means that federalism

does not represent an alternative ideology to liberalism, democracy and socialism which, having promoted and organized the liberation of the middle class, the lower middle class and the working class, over the course of history became rivals—each of them excluding the others—thus obstructing the realization of their respective values of freedom and equality, which as such are complementary and not alternative. As a result, federalism does not need to smother liberalism, democracy and socialism in order to grow; on the contrary, federalism can thrive only by cooperating to complete the achievement of freedom and equality through peace, for which only federalism can provide the appropriate moral, institutional and historical setting (Albertini M., 1999, 181–182).

Federalism plays thus in our time a role similar to that played in the past by the liberal, democratic and socialist ideologies: by its elaboration and establishment of a culture of peace, it proposes a project of society able to give an answer to the major problems of our time, and reopens the possibility to think the future, which had grown dim in traditional ideologies due to the exhaustion of their revolutionary thrust.

7.4 WORLD FEDERALISM

The era of the world wars ended with the nuclear explosions on Hiroshima and Nagasaki. From that moment the nuclear era started, which is the expression of a new condition of humanity: the loss of its immortality. As a result of this, the history of man can be divided into two periods: the pre-nuclear era, in which only nature had the power of destroying civilization and the human species, and the nuclear era, in which man has acquired the power to extinguish its own species and to interrupt the continuation of life on this planet. Einstein (1879–1955) wrote that "the releasing of the atom's power has changed everything but our way of thinking; so we are drifting away towards an unprecedented catastrophe" (Nathan O., Norden H., 1960, 376). Actually, nuclear weapons have been built as war instruments in a world of sovereign States. The dilemma the human kind is confronted with is the choice between a global political revolution or extinction. *One World or None*: this was the title of a book published in the United States in 1946, which was collecting the contributions by several intellectuals and scientists, including Einstein, whose purpose was to illustrate the dramatic alternative looming on mankind's future (Masters D., Way K. (eds.), 1946).

Hobbes had stressed that the end of the institution of the state was the conservation of life, the protection of individuals from the danger of a violent death. In the nuclear era, the state has lost that power. For the first time in history, the ancient dream of universal peace is imposing itself with the urgency of a necessity to be pursued immediately, in order to cope with the common danger of a catastrophe looming on the entire human kind. In other terms, peace is imposing itself as the priority objective, because we have to assert mankind's interests as something superior to those of classes and nations.

The advancement of science and technology has started off enormous transformations in the social, political and cultural fields. On the one hand, the progress in communication and transportation, the rise of a worldwide market, the internationalization of the production process have made the world interdependent and the national borders obsolete. For the first time in history, the world has become a unity. But it is, so far, a negative unity only. In fact, man has acquired the power to destroy the world, but not yet that of governing it. In the face of the global character and the destructive potential of world wars, Kant's project of perpetual peace through a world federation does not appear any longer as a distant ultimate end of universal history, but takes on the character of the concrete proposal able to offer a practical solution to the immediate problems afflicting mankind.

In 1947 in Montreux the World Movement for the World Federal Government was constituted, a movement which spread mostly in the Western world, but present also to a significant extent in Japan, India and Latin America. It had liaisons with the first mundialist movements born after the first World War, which had started differentiating themselves from the pacifist ones for their criticism of the limits of the League of Nations and for their proposal of a world federation, seen as an instrument for taking away from the States the monopoly of coercive power and for eliminating war. Addressing the same criticism to the UN, the World Federalist Movement (this is the name the Movement took in 1991) in the second post-war period chose two different strategic approaches: one that, ignoring the UN, was pointing to a big quality leap that would cause the immediate passage from the division of the world in sovereign states to the world federation, and the other having the objective to reform the UN, so as to strengthen and democratise that institution.

The Anatomy of Peace by Emery Reves (1904–1985), published in June 1945, the book of a federal inspiration that had the largest circulation in the 20th century, belongs to the first approach. It contains, in tune with Kant's idea of war and peace, a simple and clear message: in order to outlaw war, a radical transformation of international relations is necessary, such as to bring about a permanent and universal union of all peoples under the authority of a world government, allowing every state to renounce war as an instrument for defending its interests.

According to Reves, the scientific revolution, brought up in the agenda by the topical importance of world federalism, is similar to the Copernican revolution.

We are living in a geocentric world of nation-states. We look upon economic, social and political problems as "national" problems. No matter in which country we live, the centre of our political universe is our own nation. In our outlook, the immovable point around which all other nations, all the problems and events outside our nation, the rest of the world, supposedly rotate, is our nation. [. . .] Our political and social conceptions are Ptolemaic. The world in which we live is Copernican. Our Ptolemaic political conceptions in a Copernican industrial world are bankrupt [. . .]. There is not the slightest hope that we can possibly solve any of the vital problems of our generation until we rise above dogmatic nation-centric conceptions and realise that, in order to understand the political, economic and social problems of this highly integrated and industrialised world, we have to shift our standpoint and see all nations and national matters in motion, in their interrelated functions, rotating according to the same laws, without any fixed point created by our own imagination for our own convenience (Reves E., 34–35).

The nation-centric paradigm looks at politics from the standpoint of national interest and not from that of humankind's common interest. In an anarchical world, dominated by the conflict among many national interests, no universal interest can emerge, only the clash among national interests and the hegemony of the strongest. This means that the nation-centred paradigm belongs to the culture of violence and war.

The criticism of the limits of the UN voices the same objections that the federalist cultural tradition addressed to the confederal institutions: the UN is simply a multilateral treaty, which puts no limitation to the states' sovereignty. Paraphrasing a famous sentence by Hamilton, Reves says that

to believe that we can maintain peace among men living in separate, sovereign national unities by the method of diplomacy and policy, without government, without the creation of sovereign lawmaking, independent judiciary and executive institutions expressing the sovereignty of the people and equally binding for all, is a mere dream (Reves E., 136).

Peace requires first of all that the powers indispensable to forbid the use of force by the states and to enforce a world law on all states and all individuals, and, secondly, that legislative, executive and juridical institutions be built that ensure legal order and democracy within individual states.

The weakest aspect of Reves' proposal is the idea that the world government can be established without involving the UN. Reves does not believe that the United Nations can represent a first step towards a better international order. In his postscript to *The Anatomy of Peace* he argues that "world government *is* the first step" (Reves E., 244). His assumption is that intermediate stages are unthinkable between a system of sovereign states and a world federation. The model Reves takes inspiration from is that of the Philadelphia Convention, which in four months drafted the Constitution of the United States. It is a model which, as the European unification process shows on a smaller scale, is not applicable to the building of a world federation.

The international context in which proposals of this kind, based on the assumption that it is possible to immediately get a world Constitution drafted by a world constituent assembly, could still have some chance of success, was the immediate post-war period. In those years it was still possible to cherish the illusion that the alliance between the United States and the Soviet Union could continue even after the defeat of Germany. It dates to 1948 the *Preliminary Draft of a World Constitution*, prepared by the Chicago Committee. Members of the committee were the Italian writer, exile in the United States, Giuseppe A. Borgese (1882–1952) and his wife Elisabeth Mann (1918–2002), daughter of Thomas Mann (1876–1955)—who in 1943 took a stand in favour of the European federation and in 1949 wrote the introduction to the German translation of the *Preliminary Draft*—and other renowned academics like Robert Hutchins (1899–1955), Mortimer Adler (1903–2001) and Charles McIlwain (1871–1968).

The proposed Constitution was instituting a Federal Republic of the World, hence a state by full right, endowed with vast competences for making it capable of pursuing not only the objective to maintain peace, but also to intervene into a state territory in case human rights were violated or the republican order was jeopardized; to regulate commerce and international migrations; and to manage public transport on the world scale. At the base of the constitutional architecture of the Republic of the World there is the federal Assembly elected by universal suffrage with the proportion of one delegate every one million inhabitants. However, to this large body is awarded only the constituent power, to be exercised every nine years, but not the legislative power. The Assembly meets every three years and acts as electoral body for electing the President, the holder of the executive power, who stays in office six years, and the legislative (one-chamber) Council, which stays in office three years. Before proceeding to the election to the above posts, the assembly splits in nine electoral constituencies to nominate the candidates among whom the President and the 99 members of the Council shall be chosen. These constituencies correspond to nine big regions of the world, which foreshadow an intermediate government level between the states and the world. The Great Tribunal, appointed and presided over by the President, is composed of 60 judges, who stay in office 15 years. It has functions of control over the other powers of the Republic. When it performs its normal judicial functions, it splits in five Tribunals. The Tribune of the people is the spokesman of minorities. Finally, the Chamber of the guardians, endowed with the control and the use of the armed forces, is presided over by the President and composed of other six members elected every three years in a joint session of the legislative Council and the Great Tribunal.

This charming institutional construction, despite the doubts that some choices may arise (the excessive number of the members of the federal

Assembly, the indirect election of the legislative Assembly, the one-chamber Parliament, etc.), constitutes one of the possible answers to the political and intellectual challenge of thinking of a world government. Having thought it out constitutes, apart from the feasibility of the institutions as devised, an act of faith in reason.

The other approach that has characterized the commitment for a world federation has the objective to reform the UN by endowing it with supra-national powers, limited but real, and by democratizing it. It is a seemingly realistic approach, because it rests on existing world institutions and tries to reform them according to the model of constitutional gradualism, successfully experimented in the European Community. The book by G. Clark and L. B. Sohn (1914–2006) *World Peace through World Law* (1958) contains a real project for revising the UN Charter, drawn up in the form of amendments to its individual articles. The plan was proposing to institute within the UN a limited world government, but strong enough to be able to pursue the objective of peace. Hence the world government is not conceived as an institution provided with all the powers which are normally awarded to federations. On the contrary, it had to have competences exclusively limited to pursuing the objective of maintaining peace.

The project was proposing a general disarmament (the control of which was given to a world police force, that should be provided with equipment adequate to maintaining peace), the UN membership for all the states with no right of secession, the abolition of the right of veto. The institutional reform provided for the transformation of the General Assembly in a one-chamber world Parliament, where each member should represent five million citizens. The executive power should be awarded to the Security Council, to which the Assembly should give and repeal its confidence; finally, to the world Court binding jurisdictional powers should be granted, to enforce international law on both states and individuals.

These reforms would have instituted an embryo of a federal world government. As time went by, the authors realized that without competences in the economic field the world peace would have met serious dangers and acknowledged the necessity to institute an authority for world development. However, Clark's and Sohn's constitutional minimalism can be interpreted as an attempt to define a limited reform of the UN institutions, such as to change the overall political situation and create thus the preconditions for a deeper reform. The fact remains that the cold war made it impossible to make any progress in this direction too.

Hans Kelsen's (1881–1973) most significant contribution to federalist thinking consists in a reflection on the transition to the world government. He shares Kant's standpoint that the essential aim of law is peace. For ensuring a universal and permanent peace and for eliminating war it is necessary

> to unite all individual states [. . .] in a world state, to concentrate all their means of power, their armed forces, and put them at the disposal of a world government under laws created by a world parliament. If states are allowed to continue their existence only as members of a powerful world federation, then peace among them will be secured as effectively as among the component States of the United States of America or the Cantons of the Swiss Republic (Kelsen H., 1944, 5).

However, Kelsen tries to place this project in history and in particular in the context of the negotiations among big powers, that would lead, after the end of World War Two, to the institution of the UN. The book *Peace through Law* was published in 1944, one year before the institution of the UN, but already then Kelsen could say with certainty:

> At present, however, such a world state is not within the scope of political reality, for it is also incompatible with 'the principle of equal sovereignty' upon which, according to the Declaration signed by the governments of the United States, the United Kingdom, the Soviet Union and China on November 1, 1943, at Moscow, the international organization to be established after the war shall be based (Kelsen H., 1944, 12).

Thus, Kelsen moves his attention to the transition process towards the world state. "From a strategic point of view," he says, "there is but one serious question: What is the next step to be taken on this road?" (Kelsen H., 1944, 12). A political design, however noble and important it is in its desire to improve the conditions of human life, remains confined in the realm of dreams if the possible routes are not found for its implementation. He stresses the strange similarity between the anarchy in primitive communities and that of the international community. On this similarity he bases the assumption that the transition from primitive society to the state offers a guiding criterion with regard to the evolution of the international community. In other terms, the transition to the world federation is a long-term process comparable with the formation of the state, which consisted in a continuous process of power concentration.

> Long before parliaments as legislative bodies come into existence—he wrote— courts were established to apply the law to concrete cases. It is interesting to note that the meaning of the word 'parliament' was originally court. In primitive society the courts were hardly more than tribunals of arbitration. They had to decide only whether or not the crime had actually been committed as claimed by

one party, and hence, if the conflict could not be settled by peaceful agreement, whether or not one party was authorized to execute a sanction against the other according to the principle of self-defence. Only at a later stage did it become possible completely to abolish the procedure of self-defence and to replace it by execution of the court-decision through a centralized executive power, a police force of the state. The centralization of executive power is the last step in this evolution from the decentralized pre-state community to the centralized community we call state. [This is his conclusion]: We have good reason to believe that international law [. . .] develops in the same way as the primitive law of the pre-state community (Kelsen H., 1944, 21–22).

Kelsen assumes that the creation of an international Court represents the first step on the road leading to the world federation. The institution of an International Criminal Court in 1998 seems to be a confirmation of that assumption. It is the sign that the world is approaching an order in which the subjects of international law are the individuals, and no longer the states only. Also the institutional evolution of the European institutions confirms this assumption. The first European Community institution which asserted itself as a supranational power was the Court of Justice; then the European Parliament, as a result of its direct election, increased its powers and progressively asserted itself as a supra-national legislative assembly; in the end the governing power of the European Commission will come.

There is however one aspect of Kelsen's conception which today looks outdated: he sees the world federation as a federation of nation-states. He does not consider any intermediate government level between the national and the world government. The limit of this proposal lies in the fact that it does not solve the problem of inequality among states, which is the cause of one of the most serious flaws of the UN General Assembly, because it implies the equalization of city-states, like San Marino, with states as large as a great region of the world, like China. The subsidiarity principle would require that the nation-states be represented at macro-regional level and that these, in turn, be represented at world level.

The bipolar world order, formed after World War Two, was dominated by the strong rivalry between the United States and the Soviet Union, and by the armaments race. The UN, lacking powers of its own, was paralysed by the cross-vetoes between the two superpowers, which tried to favour the thrust by the productive forces towards the establishment of a global economy and a global society, promoting the design of world unification under the flag, respectively, of democracy and communism. During the cold war, neither the project of disarmament nor that of UN reform made any progress. In that period international policy was guided by the doctrine of nuclear dissuasion, which constitutes an attempt to overcome the limits of the traditional military doctrine, become anachronistic because of the discovery of nuclear weapons. The theory of dissuasion acknowledges that nuclear weapons are so destructive that, should they be used, there will be neither winners nor losers. However, it represents the attempt to justify nuclear weapons: to the balance of terror is assigned the function to avert war. It has, however, a big flaw, observed by Jonathan Schell (born in 1943):

> If we try to guarantee our safety by threatening ourselves with doom, then we have to mean the threat; but if we mean it, then we are actually planning to do, in some circumstance or other, that which we categorically must never do and are supposedly trying to prevent—namely, extinguish ourselves. This is the circularity at the core of the nuclear deterrence doctrine; we seek to avoid our self-extinction by threatening to perform the act (Schell J., 201).

In the light of the theory of deterrence there is no sound reason why the conflicting parties should not launch the first strike. It is a doctrine that cannot meet the target it was devised for: it lets the destructive potential of nuclear weapons co-exist with the old system of national sovereignties. Schell underlines that the scope of nuclear weapons is to defend national interests and sovereignties:

> Sovereignty is the 'reality' that the 'realists' counsel us to accept as inevitable , referring to any alternative as 'unrealistic' or 'utopian'. If the argument about nuclear weapons is to be conducted in good faith, then just as those who favor the deterrence policy [. . .] must in all honesty admit that their scheme contemplates the extinction of man in the name of protecting national sovereignty [. . .] we are told 'realism' compels us to preserve the system of sovereignty [. . .] We are told that we must preserve sovereignty and always settle our differences with violence. If this is our fate, then it is our fate to die (Schell J., 218).

The risk of extinction is then the price to be paid by mankind in exchange for the choice to continue to remain divided in sovereign states.

Despite the fact that the overcoming of the system of sovereign States and the institution of a world government still remain distant goals, the coming to power in the Soviet Union of Mikhail Gorbachev (born in 1931) has represented a turn in contemporary conscience, because it has contributed to spread the awareness of the irrational nature of the armaments race and to establish new principles in military strategy.

> Nuclear war—Gorbachev wrote—is senseless; it is irrational. There would be neither winners nor losers in a global nuclear conflict: world civilization would inevitably perish. It is a suicide, rather than a war in the conventional sense of the word [. . .]. Clausewitz's dictum that war is the continuation of policy only

by different means, which was classical in his time has grown hopelessly out of date. It now belongs to libraries [. . .]. From the security point of view the arms race has become an absurdity, because its very logic leads to destabilizing international relations and eventually to a nuclear conflict. Diverting huge resources from other priorities, the arms race is lowering the level of security, impairing it. It is in itself an enemy of peace. The only way to security is through political decisions and disarmament. In our age genuine and equal security can be guaranteed by constantly lowering the level of the strategic balance, from which nuclear and other weapons of mass-destruction should be completely eliminated (Gorbachev M., 1988, 140).

The principle of "mutual security" is the pillar of this new political vision, since

security is indivisible. It is either equal security for all or none at all [. . .] The security of each nation should be coupled with the security for all members of the world community. [. . .][Moreover], the new outlooks influence equally strongly the character of military doctrines connected to new notions as the reasonable sufficiency of armaments, non-aggressive defence, the elimination of imbalance and asymmetries in various types of armed forces and so on" (Gorbachev M., 1988, 142–143).

Several treaties concluded between the United States and the Soviet Union for the reduction and control of nuclear, chemical and biological weapons, were inspired by this outlook, even if the plan on the elimination of all mass-destruction weapons by 2000, proposed by Gorbachev on January 15, 1986 (Gorbachev M., 1986, 9–24) is still far from being implemented.

Of course, disarmament is not the high-road leading to peace.

Universal peace—Lord Lothian said—will never come from universal disarmament. [. . .] Until the institutions of a state were established, there was no other way of settling disputed questions than fighting, and if individuals who felt themselves unjustly treated or aggrieved, had not been able to use guns they would have used clubs or their fists, or any weapon to their hands, to defend what they believed to be their rights. They cannot and they will not disarm without an alternative system of protection and of settling disputes. (Lord Lothian, *Pacifism is not Enough*, 1990, 70).

To stress the point that the problem of peace is one of an institutional nature, Lord Lothian made the assumption that fire-arms were eliminated. Even then war would not be abolished, and men would use clubs and fists for defending their rights. However, the trend to armaments limitation, and in particular to the elimination of mass-destruction weapons, shows the prevailing of a disposition to co-operation rather than rivalry, which is one of the necessary, but not sufficient, conditions for starting a transition process towards a world government. It was the unbearable cost of the armaments race that convinced the Soviet Union first, and then the United States, to stop seeking military superiority and drove both of them to pursue security through co-operation rather than in competition. The fact remains, however, that nuclear weapons can never be disinvented. And even if they were totally eliminated, there will never be the certainty that they cannot be rebuilt and used. Therefore, the road to the elimination of the nuclear threat, which the two superpowers have entered, could become irreversible only if they will simultaneously take steps towards the building of a world government. This is the only realistic answer to the dangers of nuclear proliferation that have shown up in Southern Asia and Middle East can spread to other areas of the planet.

However, the Gorbachev endeavour to promote disarmament was associated with a larger idea: that federalism can pave the way to international pacification. He stated that federalism is

> a universal principle for the building of new international relations within a new world order. [. . .] The subject of federalism is relevant not only to the former Soviet republics and the Balkans, but also to North America, Europe, India and China. So, phenomenon of federalism affects the interests of the entire global community. Here I see the grounds for the joining of efforts, not only intellectual, but also political, to comprehend these topical issues. I can also visualize a new role for the UN in this endeavour (Gorbachev M., 1994, 6–7).

If we consider the vigorous growth of the globalisation process, on the one hand it highlights the decline of the last superpower (the United States) as far as the need to govern the world market is concerned, on the other it is bound to foster the strengthening of economic, monetary, social, environmental international institutions, their co-ordination and prospectively their democratisation, following the logic that has governed the evolution of European institutions. With the process of globalization and the erosion of state sovereignty we have reached a new stage of political growth, which suggests that the nation-state "is only the *latest*, not the *last*, stage in the process of political expansion." The Mortimer Adler's fore-going quotation is particularly helpful to describe the reorganization of power in progress in the contemporary world. He noted that, "as Aristotle [. . .] thought [that process] stopped with the city-state" and Hegel "that the nation-state must be the ultimate stage of political evolution," today we have become aware that "the only limit to political expansion is the world-state" (Adler M., 1944, 205).

In the time of the crisis of the great ideological frameworks, which can no longer inspire a vision of the future, looking again over the history of federalism lets us cast a beam of light on the history of mankind. In the federalist perspective, it appears as a civilizing process in the course of which law progressively replaces violence, through a pacification of ever-larger human groups, whose ultimate outcome is the world federation, seen as the condition for perpetual peace. This pacification process is at the same time a process of extending democracy beyond the states' borders: assembly democracy allowed to pacify tribes and unify them in the city-state; representative democracy allowed to pacify cities and unify them in national states; federal democracy represents the institutional innovation allowing it to pacify nations and unify them within a federation. As the dimensions of a state become larger, also the articulation, the differentiation and the complexity of government functions increase. These government forms are not mere superstructures of changing historical and social situations, but they are the product of free acts of political innovation and stages in the struggle by reason to establish ever higher forms of political life.

We have now reached a stage in the growth of civilization—Lionel Curtis wrote—which cannot go further, and is doomed to go back, until we discover the means of passing from the national to the international state, to the state in the truest and fullest sense of that word (Curtis L., 1950, 655).

7.5 A GLIMPSE INTO THE FUTURE

The novelty of the EU lies in the fact that it represents the most successful attempt so far to build a new form of statehood at international level, even though its pace has been slow and hesitant. The EU is the most intensively regulated region of the world. Its political institutions impose restraints on what sovereign states may do in their relations with each other, and in this it shows the way to what the UN could become in the future: namely, the guardian of international law and the framework of a process of constitutionalization of international relations. The European integration process has weakened national governments and compelled them to co-operate in order to solve together the problems they were unable to cope with separately. It has created a European civil society side by side with national civil societies, and established European institutions that represent a decision-making mechanism which progressively depleted national institutions. The process has advanced to such a stage that war among European Union member states has become inconceivable. The current political debate on the Constitution shows how far the process of unification in Europe has advanced. In other words, slowly and imperfectly something like a European Federation is taking shape.

It is wholly unrealistic to plan fusion among nation-states; that is, among forms of political organization based on power centralization and international antagonism. The EU represents a rejection of such nationalism which knows no other way to pursue unification but imperialism. The EU is not and will never be a state in the traditional meaning of the word. It will rather be a federation of states. The nascent European Federation is facing the task of promoting mutual toleration and solidarity among nations. The vitality of the European unification experience springs from the attempt to reconcile unity on the one hand with the Old Continent's diversity of peoples on the other. It relies on the principle that the result of any attempt to suppress differences will be worse than from accepting them. The experience of the European Community brings ample evidence that the epoch of World Wars has passed. The enlarged EU, which now includes most central and eastern, former communist, European countries, represents the overcoming of the epoch of the Cold War.

Whereas the Cold War has favoured Europe's unification within the Western world, it hindered any progress towards the unification of the world. The world division in opposed blocks left no room to any initiative in that direction.

The end of the Cold War and the apparent inability of the US to play the role of the world's policeman and banker, have contributed to put in the world agenda the United Nations reform. In other words, the world is facing the problem of strengthening and democratizing institutions devised at the end of World War Two, which are no longer suitable for the needs of our times. The emergence of the European Union as a global player—so far only in the monetary and trade sectors—will allow international equilibria to evolve towards multilateralism. This is the condition for awarding to the UN the role of custodian of the international order, based on law instead of force.

The main lesson to be drawn from the history of international relations is that the good functioning of a system of rules is dependent upon the power balance between the actors of a system of states. If a state wields a predominant power, it can allow itself to have no respect for the rights of other states. This means that getting over the asymmetry represented by the hegemonic role played by the US in international relations can open the way to a new world order based on law.

The fact that European unification has reached the stage of giving itself a Constitution, imperfect though it is, marks the beginning of a new phase in federal organizations: that of their unification, that is to say, of a joint effort for transforming the UN into an institution destined to truly assure peace to the world. The federalists reject the idea of a Europe-fortress (i.e. of European nationalism). A victory of federalism in Europe can show that it is possible to create a union among sovereign states, divided for centuries by bloody conflicts and nationalist hatred. The European unification is not a problem concerning only one region of the world. It is a pacification process among sovereign states which starts in one region of the world, but is bound to extend itself to the whole world.

The goal of the world federation represents the meeting ground between European federalists (UEF) and world federalists (WFM). On this ground the future of federalism will be decided. It is worth underlining the fact that an agreement on the ends leaves fully open the question of which route to follow. The problem of the transition to the world federation opens fundamental questions, for many of which the solutions are not clear yet.

For sure, many of the analysis schemes and political proposals worked out in the course of the European unification process can be used for building peace in the world and for governing globalisation, i.e. for extending to the whole world the benefits of the institutions built up for governing the European unification process. The political commitment in pursuing the goal of the European Federation has represented an opportunity for carrying out an in-depth revision of the traditional political culture, which has allowed it to consider in a new perspective the great problems of the contemporary world. Moreover, the building of the European unity has led to new institutional formulas, more adequate than those of the federal states established so far to compound Europe's need of unity and the independence of its nations. It is a theoretical and practical patrimony that represents the contribution of the European federalists to the movement for a world federal government. However, as history does not repeat itself, it compels us to review our analysis schemes and our models of political action in ever-changing situations.

We have seen that the institution of the International Criminal Court represents the first success of the political commitment of world federalists. The application of international law to individuals is a principle that indisputably reproduces on the international plane a state-peculiar prerogative and is the expression of the ongoing process of constitutionalization of international relations. It is worth underlining a non-fortuitous fact: the fifteen members of the European Union have all voted in 1998 for instituting the ICC, whereas the US has voted against. It is the confirmation that the primary objective of the EU's foreign policy is the creation of an international order founded on law.

There are two more objectives for which the EU can play a key role in making the UN evolve towards reforms of a federal kind: the reform of the UN Security Council and the UN Parliamentary Assembly.

On the one hand, with its entry in the Security Council the European Union could become for the rest of the world the model of a reconciliation among nation-states and the vehicle for giving to the other regions, still divided into nation-states, the impulse towards their federal unification. The transformation of the Security Council into the Council of the great world regions offers three advantages. Firstly, all the states, and no longer the strongest ones, as is happening now, could be represented in the Security Council through their respective regional organizations. Secondly, the hegemony of the great powers and the inequality among states could be progressively overcome by reorganizing the UN in groupings of states of equivalent dimensions and power. In particular, the developing countries of Africa, the Arab world, South Asia, South-East Asia, Latin America could find in their economic and political unification the way to free themselves from their condition of dependence. Thirdly, the unjust discrimination between permanent and non-permanent members could be overcome by replacing the right of veto with the majority vote.

On the other hand, the European Union, as a laboratory of international democracy, will become the leading country of this new political formula, and will be willing to help extend that experiment to the world level. In other words, it will promote the democratization of the United Nations. The formation of a World Parliament can only be conceived of as a gradual process, as the institutional evolution of the European Parliament has shown: at the beginning it was composed of the members of the national Parliaments, then it was elected by universal suffrage, and finally it has progressively strengthened its legislative and control powers. Therefore, the UN Parliamentary Assembly should likely be the first step on the road to the democratization of the UN.

In sum, the international role of the European Union is not just that of a model, but also that of the motor of the unification of the world.

Bibliography

Adler, Mortimer. *How to Think About War and Peace*. New York: Simon and Schuster, 1944.

Agnelli, Giovanni and Attilio Cabiati (1918). *European Federation or League of Nations?* Torino: Edizioni della Fondazione Giovanni Agnelli, 1996.

Albertini, Mario. *Proudhon*. Firenze: Vallecchi, 1974.

———. *Introduzione*, in Kant, Immanuel. *La pace, la ragione e la storia*. Bologna: Il Mulino, 1985.

———. *Il federalismo*. Bologna: Il Mulino, 1993.

_____. *Lo Stato nazionale*. Bologna: Il Mulino, 1997.

_____. *Nazionalismo e federalismo*. Bologna: Il Mulino, 1999.

Albertini, Mario, Andrea Chiti-Batelli, Giuseppe Petrilli. *Storia del federalismo europeo*, edited by Edmondo Paolini. Torino: ERI, 1973.

Aron Robert and Alexandre Marc. *Principes du fédéralisme*. Paris: Le Portulan, 1948.

Baratta, Joseph P., *The Politics of World Federation*. Westport, Ct, London: Praeger, 2004, 2vols.

Beales A.C.F. *The History of Peace*. London: G. Bell and Sons, 1931.

Berle, Adolf A. Jr. *Evolving Capitalism and Political Federalism*. Pp. 68–82 in *Federalism Mature and Emergent*, edited by Arthur W. MacMahon. Garden City, N. Y.: Doubleday and Co, 1955.

Billion, Jean-Francis. *World Federalism, European Federalism and International Democracy*. New York-Ventotene: World Federalist Movement-Altiero Spinelli Institute for Federalist Studies, 2001.

Bobbio, Norberto. *Teoria generale della politica*. Torino: Einaudi, 1999.

Buchanan, Allen. *Secession*. Boulder: Westview Press, 1991.

Burke, Edmund. *Speech on Moving His Resolutions for Conciliation with the Colonies*. Vol. 2: *The Works*. Hildesheim-New York: Georg Olms Verlag, 1975.

Calhoun, John C. *A Disquisition on Government* and *A Discourse on the Constitution and Government of the United States*. In *The Papers of John C. Calhoun*. Chapel Hill: University of South Carolina Press, 2003, vol. 28.

Cappon, Lester J., ed. *The Adams-Jefferson Letters: The Complete Correspondence between Thomas Jefferson and Abigail and John Adams*. Chapel Hill, NC.:The University of North Carolina Press, 1959, 2 vols.

Cattaneo, Carlo. *Scritti politici ed epistolario*, edited by Gabriele Rosa and Jessie W. Mario. Firenze: Barbera, 1892–1901, 3 vols.

——. *Epistolario*, edited by Rinaldo Caddeo, Firenze, Barbera, 1949–1956.

——. *Dell'insurrezione di Milano nel 1848 e della successiva guerra. Memorie*. Milano: Feltrinelli, 1973.

Chabod, Federico. *Storia dell'idea di Europa*. Bari: Laterza, 1964.

Churchill, Winston S. *The Second World War*. Vol. 2: *Their Finest Hour*. London: Cassell, 1949.

Clark, Grenville and Louis B. Sohn. *World Peace through World Law*. Cambridge, Ma,: Harvard University Press, 1966.

Cloots, Anacharsis. *Bases constitutionnelles de la République du genre humain*. Paris: Convention Nationale, 1793.

Coudenhove-Kalergi, Richard. *An Idea Conquers the World*. New York: Roy Publishers, 1954.

Curry, William B. *The Case for Federal Union*. Harmondsworth: Penguin, 1939

Curtis, Lionel, ed. *The Problem of the Commonwealth*. London: Macmillan, 1916.

Curtis, Lionel. *Civitas Dei*. London: Allen & Unwin, 1950.

Dalberg-Acton, John E.E. *Nationality* (1862), in *History of Freedom and Other Essays*. London: Macmillan, 1909.

Delzell, Charles F. "The European Federalist Movement in Italy: First Phase, 1918–1947." *Journal of Modern History* 32, no. 3 (September 1960): 241–250.

Dicey Albert V. *Introduction to the Study of the Law of the Constitution*. 8th ed. London: Macmillan, 1926.

Duroselle, Jean-Baptiste. *L'idée d'Europe dans l'histoire*. Paris: Denoël, 1961.

Einaudi, Luigi. *La guerra e l'unità europea*. Bologna: Il Mulino, 1986.

Elazar, Daniel J., ed. *Federalism and Political Integration*. Lanham, New York, London: University Press of America, 1984.

Elazar, Daniel J., ed. *Federal Systems of the World: A Handbook of Federal, Confederal and Autonomy Arrangements*. Harlow, UK: Longman, 1991.

Elazar, Daniel J., *Exploring Federalism*. Toscaloosa: University of Alabama Press, 1987.

——. *Constitutionalizing Globalization. The Postmodern Revival of Confederal Arrangement*. Lanham, Boulder, New York, Oxford: Rowman & Littlefield, 1998.

——. "Il principio federale: integrazione, differenze, identità." Interview by Anna Loretoni, *Iride* 12, no. 28 (1999): 477–497.

Engels, Friedrich. *Anti-Dühring and Dialectics of Nature* (1877). Vol 25: *Marx & Engels Internet Archive*, 2000. <http://www.marxists.org/archive/marx/index.htm> (20 June 2007).

——. *Engels to J. Bloch*, London, September 21, 1890. Vol. 49: *Marx & Engels Internet Archive*, 2000. <http://www.marxists.org/archive/marx/index.htm> (20 June 2007).

———. *Engels to Conrad Schmidt*, London, October 27, 1890. Vol. 49: *Marx & Engels Internet Archive*, 2000. <http://www.marxists.org/archive/marx/index.htm> (20 June 2007).

Ferrari, Giuseppe. *La Chine et l'Europe, leur histoire et leurs traditions comparées.* Paris: Didier, 1867.

Fiske, John. *American Political Ideas Viewed from the Standpoint of Universal History.* New York and London: Harper and Brothers, 1902.

Frantz, Constantin. *Der Untergang der alten Parteien und die Parteien der Zukunft.* Berlin: M.A. Niendorf,1878.

———. *Der Föderalismus als das leitende Prinzip für die soziale, staatliche und internationale Organisation.* Mainz: Franz Kirchheim, 1879.

Friedrich, Carl J. *Trends of Federalism in Theory and Practice.* London: Pall Mall Press, 1968.

Gorbachev, Mikhail S. *Nuclear Disarmament by the Year 2000.* Pp. 9–24 in *The Coming Century of Peace.* New York: Richardson & Steirman, 1986.

———. *Perestroika.* London: Fontana/Collins, 1988.

———. *On New Federalism.* In *Federalism and the New World Order*, edited by Stephen J.Randall and Roger Gibbins. Calgary: University of Calgary Press, 1994.

Gravier, Jean-François. *L'aménagement du territoire et l'avenir des régions françaises.* Paris: Flammarion, 1964.

Gurvitch, Georges. *Proudhon et Marx.* In *L'actualité de Proudhon.* Bruxelles: Université Libre de Bruxelles, Éditions de l'Institut de Sociologie, 1967.

Habermas, Jürgen. *The Inclusion of the Other.* Cambridge, Ma: MIT Press, 1998.

Haegler, Rolf P. *Histoire et idéologie du mondialisme.* Zürich: Europa Verlag, 1972.

Hamilton, Alexander. *The Papers of Alexander Hamilton.* New York: Columbia University Press, 1961–1979, 26 vols.

Hamilton, Alexander, John Jay , James Madison. *The Federalist* (1788). New York: The Colonial Press, 1901.

Hegel, Georg W.F. *Die Vernunft in der Geschichte. Einleitung in die Philosophie der Weltgeschichte.* Leipzig: Felix Meiner, 1917.

———. *Philosophy of Right.* Kitchener, Canada: Batoche Books, 2001.

Held, David. *Democracy and the Global Order.* London: Polity Press, 1995.

Héraud, Guy. *Popoli e lingue d'Europa.* Milano: Ferro, 1966.

Hobbes, Thomas. *Leviathan.* Cambridge: Cambridge University Press, 1904.

Höffe, Otfried. *Demokratie im Zeitalter der Globalisierung.* München: Beck, 1999.

Hugo, Victor. *Actes et paroles, avant l'exil, 1841–1851.* Paris: Michel Lévy, 1875.

Iglesias, Fernando A. *Globalizar la democracia. Por un Parlamento Mundial.* Buenos Aires: Manantial, 2006.

Junius (Luigi Einaudi). *Lettere politiche.* Bari: Laterza, 1920.

Kant, Immanuel. *Die Religion innerhalb der Grenzen der Blossen Vernunft.* Vol. 6: *Gesammelte Werke* (Akademie Ausgabe). Berlin: de Gruyter, 1914.

———. *Perpetual Peace and Other Essays*, edited. by Ted Humphrey. Indianapolis: Hackett, 1988.

Kelsen, Hans. *Peace through Law.* Chapel Hill, NC: University of North Carolina Press, 1944.

‍‌‍‍‍‌‌‍‌‍

———. *General Theory of Law and State*. Union, N.J.: The Lawbook Exchange, 1999.

King, Bolton. *Mazzini*. London-New York: J.M. Dent-E.P. Dutton, 1902.

Kimber, Charles. "The Birth of Federal Union", *The Federalist Debate* 18, no. 1 (March 2005): 10–14.

Lafont, Robert. *La révolution régionaliste*. Paris: Gallimard, 1967.

Lange, Christian L. "Histoire de la doctrine pacifique et de son influence sur le développement du droit international." *Académie de droit international, Recueil des cours* 13, no. 3 (1926): 171–426.

Lenin, Vladimir I. *On the Slogan for the United States of Europe* (1915). Pp. 339–343, vol. 21: *Collected Works*. London: Lawrence & Wishart, 1964.

———. *State and Revolution*. Vol. 25: *Collected Works*. London: Lawrence & Wishart, 1964.

———. *Declaration of Rights of the Working and Exploited People* (1918). Pp. 423–425, vol. 26: *Collected Works*. London: Lawrence & Wishart, 1964.

Lord Lothian, (Philip Kerr), *Pacifism is not Enough* (1935). London-New York: Lothian Foundation Press, 1990.

———. *The Ending of Armageddon* (1939). Pp. 1–15 in *Studies in Federal Planning*, edited by Patrick Ransome. London, New York: Lothian Foundation Press, 1990.

L'Europe de demain, edited by Centre d'action pour la fédération européenne. Neuchâtel: La Baconnière, 1945.

L'Ordre Nouveau. Aosta: Le Château, 1997, reprint edition, 5 vols.

McMaster, James B. and Frederick Stone, eds. *Pennsylvania and the Federal Constitution. 1787–1788*. Lancaster, Pa: Inquirer Printing, 1888.

Marc, Alexandre. *Dialectique du déchaînement. Fondements philosophiques du fédéralisme*. Paris: Colombe, 1961.

———. *L'Europe dans le monde*. Paris: Payot, 1965.

Marini, Giuliano. *Tre studi sul cosmopolitismo kantiano*. Pisa-Roma: Istituti editoriali e poligrafici internazionali, 1998.

Mario Jessie W. *Della vita di Giuseppe Mazzini*. Milano: Sonzogno, 1886.

Marx, Karl. *Outlines of the Critique of Political Economy. The Grundrisse (1857–1858), Notebook V*. Vol. 29: *Marx & Engels Internet Archive*, 2000. <http://www.marxists.org/archive/marx/index.htm> (20 June 2007).

Marx, Karl. *A Contribution to the Critique of Political Economy. Preface*. Vol. 29: *Marx & Engels Internet Archive*, 2000. <http://www.marxists.org/archive/marx/index.htm> (20 June 2007).

Marx, Karl and Friedrich Engels. *German Ideology* (1846). Vol. 5: *Marx & Engels Internet Archive*, 2000. <http://www.marxists.org/archive/marx/index.htm> (20 June 2007).

Masters, Dexter and Katahrine Way, eds. *One World or None*. New York: McGrow-Hill, 1946.

Mayne, Richard, John Pinder, John Roberts. *Federal Union: The Pioneers*. London: Macmillan, 1990.

Mazzini, Giuseppe. *Edizione nazionale degli scritti*. Imola: Cooperativa tipografico-editoriale Paolo Galeati, 1906–1973, 106 vols.

Monnet, Jean. *Memoirs*. London: Collins, 1978.

Montani, Guido. *Il federalismo, l'Europa e il mondo*. Manduria: Lacaita, 1999.

Nathan, Otto and Heinz Norden. *Einstein on Peace*. New York: Simon and Schuster, 1960.

Olivetti, Adriano. *L'ordine politico delle comunità* (1945). Milano: Comunità, 1970.

"Preliminary Draft of a World Constitution", edited by the Committee to Frame a World Constitution, *Common Cause* 1 (March 1948): 1–40.

Proudhon, Pierre-Joseph. *Théorie de l'impôt*. Paris: Dentu, 1861.

———. *Théorie de la propriété*. Paris: Librairie internationale, 1866.

———. *Correspondence*. Paris: Lacroix, 1874–1875, 14 vols.

———. *Système des contradictions économiques ou philosophie de la misère*, in *Oeuvres complètes*. Paris: Rivière, 1923.

———. *Qu'est-ce-que la propriété? Recherches sur le principe du droit et du gouvernement. Premier mémoire*. in *Oeuvres complètes*. Paris: Rivière, 1926.

———. *Contradictions politiques* in *Oeuvres complètes*. Paris: Rivière, 1952.

———. *Du principe fédératif et oeuvres diverses sur les problèmes politiques européens, Oeuvres complètes*. Paris: Rivière, 1959. English edition *The Principle of Federation*. Toronto: University of Toronto Press, 1979.

———. *De la justice dans la révolution et dans l'église*, in *Oeuvres complètes*. Genève-Paris: Slatkine, 1982.

Reves, Emery. *The Anatomy of Peace*. Harmondsworth: Penguin Books, 1947.

Richta, Radovan. *La civilisation au carrefour*. Paris: Anthropos, 1969.

Robbins, Lionel. *Economic Planning and International Order*. London: Macmillan, 1937.

———. *The Economic Causes of War*. London: Cape, 1939.

———. *Liberalism and the International Problem*. In *Politics and Economics*. London: Macmillan, 1963.

———. *Autobiography of an Economist*. London: Macmillan, 1971.

Robespierre, Maximilien de. *Discours à la Société des Jacobins*, séance extraordinaire du 12 décembre 1793, in Anacharsis Cloots, *Écrits révolutionnaires 1790–1794*. Paris: Champ libre, 1979.

Rosselli, Carlo. *Scritti dell'esilio, 1988–1992*. Torino: Einaudi, 1992, 2 vols.

Rossolillo, Francesco. *Città, territorio, istituzioni*. Napoli: Guida, 1983.

Rougemont, Denis de. *Vingt-huit siècles d'Europe*. Paris: Payot, 1961.

———. *L'avenir est notre affaire*. Paris: Stock, 1977.

Rougemont Denis de, ed. *Dictionnaire international du fédéralisme*. Bruxelles: Bruylant, 1994.

Sainte-Beuve, Charles-Augustin. *P.-J. Proudhon. Sa vie et sa correspondence. 1838–1848*. Paris: A. Costes, 1947.

Saint-Simon, Claude-Henry de and Augustin Thierry. *De la réorganisation de la société européenne*. In *Oeuvres de C.-H. de Saint-Simon*. Paris: Anthropos, 1966, vol. 1.

Schell, Jonathan. *The Fate of the Earth*. London: Cape, 1982.

Scholl, Inge. *Die weisse Rose*. Frankfurt/M.: Fischer, 1953.

Seeley, John R. *The Expansion of England* (1883). London: Macmillan, 1909, 2d ed.

———. "The United States of Europe." *Macmillan's Magazine* 23, (March 1871): 436–448, reprinted in *The Federalist* 31, no. 2 (1989): 174–195.

Spinelli, Altiero. *L'Europa non cade dal cielo*. Bologna: Il Mulino, 1960.

——. *Diario europeo*. Bologna: Il Mulino, 1989–1992, 3 vols.

Spinelli, Altiero, and Ernesto Rossi. *The Ventotene Manifesto* (1941). Ventotene, Italy: The Altiero Spinelli Institute for Federalist Studies, 1988.

Stalin, Iosif V. *Against Federalism* (1917). In *Works*. Moscow: Foreign Languages Publishing House, 1953, vol. 3.

Storeno (Ernesto Rossi). *Gli Stati Uniti d'Europa*. Lugano: Nuove Edizioni di Capolago, 1944. Anastatic reprint ed. by Sergio Pistone. Torino, CELID, 2004.

Streit, Clarence, *Union Now*. New York, London: Harper and Brothers, 1939.

Tocqueville, Alexis de. *Democracy in America* (1835–1840). New York: Vintage Books, 1954.

Trotsky, Lev D. *Der Krieg und die Internationale*. München: Futurus Verlag, 1914.

——. *Programme de paix* (1917). In *La guerre et la révolution*. Paris: Tête de feuilles, 1974, 2 vols.

——. *Disarmament and the United States of Europe* (1929). Vol. 1: *Writings of Leon Trotsky*. New York: Pathfinder Press, 1975.

Vile, Maurice J.C. *The Structure of American Federalism*. New York, London: Oxford University Press, 1962.

Voyenne, Bernard. *Histoire de l'idée fédéraliste*, Nice: Presses de l'Europe, 1976–1981, 3 vols.

Warren, Carl. *The Making of the Constitution*. Boston: Little, Brown and Co., 1928.

Wells, Herbert G. *The World Set Free, A Story of Mankind*. London: Macmillan, 1914.

——. *What is Coming? A European Forecast*. New York: Macmillan, 1916.

——. *The Idea of a League of Nations*. Boston: The Atlantic Monthly Press, 1919.

——. *The Open Conspiracy; Blue Prints for a World Revolution*. London: Gollancz, 1928.

——. *The Way the World Is Going*. Garden City, N.Y.: Doubleday, 1929.

Wheare, Kenneth C. *The Federal Government* (1946). 3rd ed. London: Oxford University Press, 1956.

——. *Modern Constitutions*. London: Oxford University Press, 1966.

Wootton, Barbara F. *Socialism and Federation* (1940). Pp. 269–298 in *Studies in Federal Planning*, edited by Patrick Ransome, London, New York: Lothian Foundation Press, 1990.

Index

Friedrich, Carl J., 95–97, 99, 102
functionalism, 121

Garibaldi, Giuseppe, 55
Gauthier, Antoine, 111
Germany: and the crisis of the
European system of states, 74;
antagonism toward France, 65, 87;
authoritarianism, 16; core of a
European union, 41; decline of
power, 58–59; defeat in World War
Two, 66, 74, 78; hope for
revolution in, 65; imperialism, 16,
65, 72, 114, 127; medieval, 98, 124;
multinational state, 41; Nazism, 77,
80, 113; parliamentary system, 14;
political unification, 39, 40, 74;
reconciliation with, after WWI, 76;
reconstruction of sovereignty after
WWII, 120; transformation into a
federation, vi
Girondists, 33, 106
Giustizia e libertà (Justice and liberty),
113–14
globalization, vi, 31, 43, 100, 139
Gorbachev, Mikhail, 137–39
Gravier, Jean-François, 107
Great Britain: anti-fascist power, 113;
British empire, 1, 61; conflict with
Germany, 74, 80; co-operation with
France in WWII, 88; core of a
European Union, 38;
decentralization, 126; decline of
power, 58, 61, 68; Franco-British
Union, 38, 87, 88; insular-type state,
21; maritime power, 21, 35, 74, 86;
member of the European
Community, 103; model of free
government, 4, 38; multinational
state, 68, 126; opposition to the
Treaty of European Union, 121;
parliamentary system, 14; peace
movements in, 54; proposal to give
back a full sovereignty to Western
Germany, 120; relations with the

United States, 4, 92, 120;
transformation of the British empire
into a federation, 60–61, 97
Greece: ancient, 10, 82, 98, 105, 124
Grey, George, 76
guaranteed social minimum, 109

Habermas, Jürgen, 26, 31
Hamilton, Alexander, 1–21, 27, 34, 72,
82, 132
Hegel, Georg Wilhelm, Friedrich, 3, 5,
16, 35, 139
Held, David, 26, 31
Héraud, Guy, 107
historical materialism, 58, 67; structure
and superstructure, 67, 97. *See also*
mode of production
Hitler, Adolf, 74, 80, 113
Hobbes, Thomas, 26, 130
Höffe, Otfried, 31
Holy Alliance, 50, 58
Holy Roman Empire, 98, 102, 104, 124
Hugo, Victor, 55
Hume, David, 3
Hutchins, Robert, 133

Ickes, Harold, 88
ideology: federalist, vii, 5, 29, 89, 95,
112–30; nationalist, v, 63, 110
Imperial Federation League. *See*
federalist movements
imperialism: federalist interpretation,
19, 86, 114, 117, 127, 141; German,
16, 65, 72, 114, 127; Marxist
interpretation, 66–67, 86
India: as a federation, v, 61, 94, 139; as
a world power, 3; multinational state,
v
industrial revolution. *See* mode of
production
institutions: and the historical process,
97–97, 110–11
international anarchy, 3, 17, 22, 23, 25,
29, 56, 72, 73, 77, 78, 83, 86,
114–15, 117, 129